THE ULTIMATE GUIDE TO COOKING
CHICKEN

THE ULTIMATE GUIDE TO COOKING
CHICKEN

A COLLECTION OF 200 STEP-BY-STEP RECIPES FROM TASTY SUMMER
SALADS TO CLASSIC ROASTS, ALL SHOWN IN OVER 900 PHOTOGRAPHS

LINDA FRASER

HERMES
HOUSE

This edition is published by Hermes House, an imprint of Anness Publishing Ltd,
Blaby Road, Wigston, Leicestershire LE18 4SE; info@anness.com

www.hermeshouse.com; www.annesspublishing.com

If you like the images in this book and would like to investigate using them for publishing, promotions
or advertising, please visit our website www.practicalpictures.com for more information.

Publisher: Joanna Lorenz
Cookery Editor: Rosemary Wilkinson
Copy Editor: Rosie Hankin
Designer: Bill Mason
Recipes: Catherine Atkinson, Alex Barker, Carla Capalbo, Maxine Clark, Andi Clevely, Christine France, Carole Handslip,
Sarah Gates, Shirley Gill, Norma MacMillan, Sue Maggs, Katherine Richmond, Jenny Stacey, Ruby Le Bois, Liz Trigg,
Hilaire Walden, Laura Washburn, Steven Wheeler
Photographers: Karl Adamson, Edward Allwright, Steve Baxter, James Duncan, John Freeman, Michelle Garrett,
Amanda Heywood, Don Last
Stylists: Madeleine Brehaut, Hilary Guy, Blake Minton, Kirsty Rawlings, Fiona Tillett
Food for Photography: Marilyn Forbes, Carole Handslip, Jane Hartshorn, Cara Hobday, Beverly LeBlanc, Wendy Lee,
Lucie McKelvie, Jenny Shapter, Elizabeth Silver, Jane Stevenson, Liz Trigg, Elizabeth Wolf-Cohen
Illustrator: Anna Koska

ETHICAL TRADING POLICY
Because of our ongoing ecological investment programme, you, as our customer, can have the pleasure and reassurance
of knowing that a tree is being cultivated on your behalf to naturally replace the materials used to make the book you
are holding. For further information about this scheme, go to www.annesspublishing.com/trees

© Anness Publishing Ltd 2011

A CIP catalogue record for this book is available from the British Library.

Previously published as *The Ultimate Chicken Cookbook*

NOTES
For all recipes, quantities are given in both metric and imperial measures and, where appropriate, in standard cups and spoons.
Follow one set of measures, but not a mixture, because they are not interchangeable.
Standard spoon and cup measures are level. 1 tsp = 5ml, 1 tbsp = 15ml, 1 cup = 250ml/8fl oz.
Australian standard tablespoons are 20ml. Australian readers should use 3 tsp in place of 1 tbsp for measuring small quantities.
American pints are 16fl oz/2 cups. American readers should use 20fl oz/2.5 cups in place of 1 pint when measuring liquids.
Electric oven temperatures in this book are for conventional ovens. When using a fan oven, the temperature will probably
need to be reduced by about 10–20°C/20–40°F. Since ovens vary, you should check with your manufacturer's
instruction book for guidance.
Medium (US large) eggs are used unless otherwise stated.

Main front cover image shows Chicken with Lemon and Herbs, substituting chicken fillets
for the chicken thighs – for recipe, see page 150.

PUBLISHER'S NOTE

CONTENTS

~

Introduction

Chicken is popular with children and adults alike. It is versatile and economical, and can be cooked with a wide variety of ingredients and flavours. It is low in fat and quick to cook, with very little wastage.

Chicken can be bought in many forms: whole, quartered or jointed into thighs, drumsticks, breasts and wings, with or without bones and skin, which makes preparation very easy. Minced chicken can be found at some large supermarkets, but the skinned flesh can be minced quickly in a food processor. Although it is convenient to buy portions individually packed, it is expensive. It is much cheaper to buy a whole chicken and prepare it yourself and cheaper still to buy a frozen chicken and defrost it thoroughly before using. To get the best results from a frozen bird, allow it to thaw slowly in a cool place overnight or until completely defrosted. Many types of chicken are available, such as free-range and corn-fed (with yellow skin) and all are full of flavour. Some have added herbs and flavourings, and others are self-basting with either butter or olive oil injected into the flesh. This helps to keep the flesh succulent. Baby chickens are called poussins and can be bought to serve whole or halved depending on their size. In fact, chicken can be bought at any weight from 450g to 2.75kg (1lb to 6lb) to suit the size of your family.

The recipes in this book are mostly based on a family of four people, but they can be easily halved for two or doubled for eight. There are chapters on soups, salads and pies as well as one pot meals, midweek meals and hot and spicy dishes to provide you with a best-ever chicken meal for every occasion.

Choosing a Chicken

A fresh chicken should have a plump breast and the skin should be creamy in colour. The tip of the breast bone should be pliable.

A bird's dressed weight is taken after plucking and drawing and may include the giblets (neck, gizzard, heart and liver). A frozen chicken must be thawed slowly in the fridge or a cool room. Never put it in hot water, as this will toughen the flesh and is dangerous as it allows bacteria to multiply.

Poussins
These are four to six weeks old and weigh 450g–550g/1–1¹/4lb. One is enough for one person.

Double poussins
These are eight to ten weeks old and weigh 800–900g/1³/4–2lb. One will serve two people. Poussins are best roasted, grilled or pot-roasted.

Boilers
These are about twelve months and over and weigh between 2–3kg/4–6lb. They require long, slow cooking, around 2–3 hours, to make them tender.

Roasters
These birds are about six to twelve months old and weigh 1.5–2kg/3–4lb. One will feed a family.

Corn-fed chickens
These are generally more expensive. They usually weigh 1.25–1.5kg/2¹/2–3lb.

Spring chickens
These birds are about three months old and weigh 900g–1.25kg/2–2¹/2lb. One will serve three to four people.

Cuts of Chicken

Chicken pieces are available pre-packaged in various forms. If you do not want to buy a whole bird, you can make your choice from the many selected cuts on the market.

Some cooking methods are especially suited to specific cuts of poultry.

Drumstick
The drumstick is a firm favourite for barbecuing or frying, either in batter or rolled in breadcrumbs.

Wing
The wing does not supply much meat, and is often barbecued or fried.

Liver
This makes a wonderful addition to pâtés or to salads.

Skinless boneless thigh
This makes tasks such as stuffing and rolling much quicker, as it is already skinned and jointed.

Thigh
The thigh is suitable for casseroling and other slow-cooking methods.

Breast
The tender white meat can be simply cooked in butter, or can be stuffed for extra flavour.

Minced chicken
This is not as strongly flavoured as, say, ground beef but it may be used as a substitute in some recipes.

Leg
This comprises the drumstick and thigh. Large pieces with bones, such as this, are suitable for slow-cooking, such as casseroling or poaching.

Trussing Poultry

Trussing holds a bird together during cooking so that it keeps a neat, attractive shape. If the bird is stuffed, trussing prevents the stuffing falling out. You can truss with strong string or with poultry skewers.

An alternative to the method shown here is to use a long trussing needle and fine cotton string: make two passes, in alternate directions, through the body at the open end, from wing to wing, and tie. Then pass the needle through the parson's nose and tie the string around the ends of the drumsticks.

Remove trussing before serving.

1 For an unstuffed bird: set it breast down and pull the neck skin over the neck opening. Turn the bird breast up and fold each wing tip back, over the skin, to secure firmly behind the shoulder.

2 Press the legs firmly down and into the breast. If there is a band of skin across the parson's nose, fold back the ends of the drumsticks and tuck them under the skin.

3 Otherwise, cross the knuckle ends of the drumsticks or bring them tightly together. Loop a length of string several times around the drumstick ends, tie a knot and trim off excess string.

4 For a stuffed bird: fold the wing tips back as above. After stuffing the neck end, fold the flap of skin over the opening and secure it with a skewer, then fold over the wing tips.

5 Put any stuffing or flavourings (herbs, lemon halves, apple quarters and so on) in the body cavity, then secure the ends of the drumsticks as above, tying in the parson's nose, too.

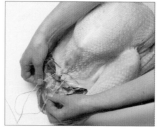

6 Or, the cavity opening can be closed with skewers: insert two or more skewers across the opening, threading them through the skin several times.

7 Lace the skewers together with string. Tie the drumsticks together over the skwers.

STUFFING TIPS

Only use stuffing that is cool, not hot or chilled. Pack it loosely in the bird and cook any leftovers separately. Stuff poultry just before cooking. Do not stuff the body cavity of a large bird because this could inhibit heat penetration, and thus harmful bacteria may not be destroyed.

Roasting Poultry

Where would family gatherings be without the time-honoured roast bird? But beyond the favourite chicken, all types of poultry can be roasted – from small poussins to large turkeys. However, older tougher birds are better pot-roasted.

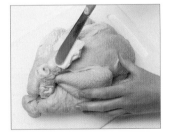

1 Wipe the bird inside and out with damp kitchen paper, stuff, if directed, and truss it. Spread the breast of chicken with soft butter or oil; bard a lean game bird; prick the skin of duck or goose.

2 Set the bird breast up on a rack in a small roasting tin or shallow baking dish. If you are roasting a lean game bird, set the bird in the tin breast down.

3 Roast the bird, basting every 10 minutes after the first 30 minutes with the juices and fat in the tin. Turn if directed. If browning too quickly, cover with foil.

4 Put the bird on a carving board and leave to rest for at least 15 minutes before serving. Meanwhile make a simple sauce or gravy with the juices in the tin.

ROASTING TIMES FOR POULTRY

Note: Cooking times given here are for unstuffed birds.
For stuffed birds, add 20 minutes to the total roasting time.

POUSSIN	450–700g/1–1^1/2lb	1–1^1/4 hours at 180°C/350°F/Gas 4
CHICKEN	1.12–1.35kg/2^1/2–3lb	1–1^1/4 hours at 190°C/375°F/Gas 5
	1.5–1.8kg/3^1/2–4lb	1^1/4–2 hours at 190°C/375°F/Gas 5
	2.2–2.25kg/4^1/2–5lb	1^1/2–2 hours at 190°C/375°F/Gas 5
	2.25–2.7kg/5–6lb	1^3/4–2^1/2 hours at 190°C/375°F/Gas 5
DUCK	1.35–2.25kg/3–5lb	1^3/4–2^1/4 hours at 200°C/400°F/Gas 6
GOOSE	3.6–4.5kg/8–10lb	2^1/2–3 hours at 180°C/350°F/Gas 4
	4.5–5.4kg/10–12lb	3–3^1/2 hours at 180°C/350°F/Gas 4
TURKEY	2.7–3.6kg/6–8lb	3–3^1/2 hours at 160°C/325°F/Gas 3
(whole bird)	3.6–5.4kg/8–12lb	3–4 hours at 160°C/325°F/Gas 3
	5.4–7.2kg/12–16lb	4–5 hours at 160°C/325°F/Gas 3
TURKEY	1.8–2.7kg/4–6lb	1^1/2–2^1/4 hours at 160°C/325°F/Gas 3
(whole breast)	2.7–3.6kg/6–8lb	2^1/4–3^1/4 hours at 160°C/325°F/Gas 3

Jointing Poultry

Although chickens and other poultry are sold already jointed into halves, quarters, breasts, thighs and drumsticks, sometimes it makes sense to buy a whole bird and to do the job yourself. That way you can prepare four larger pieces or eight smaller ones, depending on the recipe, and you can cut the pieces so the backbone and other bony bits (which can be saved for stock) are not included. In addition, a whole bird is cheaper to buy than pieces.

A sharp knife and sturdy kitchen scissors or poultry shears make the job of jointing poultry very easy.

1 With the sharp knife, cut through the skin on one side of the body down to where the thigh joins the body. Bend the leg out away from the body and twist it to break the ball and socket joint.

2 Hold the leg out away from the body and cut through the ball and socket joint, taking the "oyster meat" from the backbone with the leg. Repeat on the other side.

3 To separate the breast from the back, cut through the flap of skin just below the rib cage, cutting towards the neck. Pull the breast and back apart, cutting through the joints that connect them. Reserve the back for stock.

4 Turn the whole breast over, skin side down. Take one side of the breast in each hand and bend back firmly so the breastbone pops free. Loosen the bone on both sides with your fingers and using a knife to help, remove it.

5 Cut the breast lengthways in half, cutting through the wishbone. You now have 2 breasts with wings attached and 2 leg portions.

6 For 8 pieces, cut each breast in half at an angle so that some breast is included with each wing. Trim off any protruding bones.

7 With the knife, cut each leg portion through the ball and socket joint to separate the thigh and drumstick.

TERMS FOR
CHICKEN
BREASTS

If the wing is left attached to the chicken breast, this is termed a "supreme". If the breast is completely boned, it is called a "fillet".

Boning a Chicken

For the purpose of stuffing and to make carving simple, it is essential to bone a chicken. Use a sharp knife with a short blade. Work in short, scraping movements, keeping the knife against the bone at all times, to leave the carcass clean.

This is a fiddly job, so allow yourself plenty of time.

Save the chicken bones, which will be ideal for making chicken stock.

1 Remove any trussing string. Cut off the wing tips (pinions) and discard. With a short-bladed, sharp knife cut the skin along the underside (backbone) of the chicken. Carefully work the skin and flesh away from the carcass with the knife until the leg joints are exposed.

2 Cut the sinew between the ball and socket joints. This sinew joins the thigh bones and wings to the carcass.

3 Holding the rib cage away from the chicken body, carefully scrape the breastbone clean and cut the carcass away from the skin. Take great care not to cut through the skin, or the stuffing will burst out of the hole.

4 Take hold of the thigh bone in one hand, and with the knife scrape the flesh down the bone to the next joint.

5 Cut around the joint and continue cleaning the drumstick until the whole leg bone is free. Repeat with the other leg and both the wings. Lay the chicken flat and turn the flesh of the legs and wings inside the chicken. Flatten the flesh neatly ready for stuffing.

HANDLING RAW POULTRY
◡

Raw poultry may harbour harmful organisms, such as salmonella bacteria, so it is vital to take care in its preparation. Always wash your hands, chopping board, knife and poultry shears in hot soapy water before and after handling poultry. If possible use a chopping board that can be washed at high temperature in a dishwasher and always keep a chopping board just for the preparation of raw poultry. Thaw frozen poultry completely before cooking.

Spatchcocking Poultry

Whole chickens, poussins, guinea fowl and game birds can be split in half and opened up flat like a book, to resemble the wings of a butterfly. They will then cook evenly under the grill or on a barbecue. A heavy chef's knife can be used to split the bird, but sturdy kitchen scissors or poultry shears are easier to handle.

1 Set the bird breast down. Cut through the skin and rib cage along one side of the backbone, working from the tail end to the neck. Repeat on the other side of the backbone to cut it free. Keep the backbone for stock, if wished.

2 Turn the bird breast up. With the heel of your hand, press firmly on the breastbone to break it and flatten the breast.

TESTING POULTRY

Overcooked poultry is dry, tough and tasteless, so knowing when a bird is done is crucial. The most reliable test for a whole bird is to insert a meat thermometer deep into the thigh meat (the internal temperature should be 79°C/175°F). Without a thermometer, you can test by piercing the thigh with a skewer or the tip of a knife; the juices that run out should be clear, not pink. Or lift the bird with a long two-pronged fork and tilt it so you can check the colour of the juices that run out of the cavity into the roasting tin. Pieces of poultry, particularly breasts, can be tested by pressing them with a finger; the meat should be firm but still slightly springy.

3 Fold the wing tips back behind the shoulders. Thread a long metal skewer through one wing and the top of the breast and out through the other wing.

4 Thread a second skewer through the thighs and bottom of the breast. These skewers will keep the bird flat during cooking, and will make it easy to turn over.

GRILLING TIMES FOR POULTRY

Note: Cook 10–15cm/4–6in from the heat; thinner pieces, less than 2.5cm/1in nearer the heat. If the poultry seems to be browning too quickly, turn down the heat slightly.

POUSSIN, SPATCHCOCKED	20–25 minutes
SPRING CHICKEN, SPLIT IN HALF OR SPATCHCOCKED	25–30 minutes
ROASTING CHICKEN, SPLIT IN HALF OR SPATCHCOCKED	30–40 minutes
CHICKEN BREAST, DRUMSTICK, THIGH	30–35 minutes
SKINLESS BONELESS CHICKEN BREAST	10–12 minutes
BONELESS DUCK BREAST	10–12 minutes

Making Poultry Stock

A good home-made poultry stock is invaluable in the kitchen. It is simple and economical to make, and can be stored in the freezer for up to 6 months. If poultry giblets are available, add them (except the livers) with the wings.

INGREDIENTS

Makes about 2.5 litres/4 pints/10 cups

1.12–1.35kg/2^1/$_2$–3lb poultry wings, backs and necks (chicken, turkey, etc)

2 onions, unpeeled, quartered

4 litres/7 pints cold water

2 carrots, roughly chopped

2 celery stalks, with leaves if possible, roughly chopped

a small handful of fresh parsley

a few fresh thyme sprigs or

^{3}/$_4$ tsp dried thyme

1 or 2 bay leaves

10 black peppercorns, lightly crushed

1 Combine the poultry wings, backs and necks and the onions in a stockpot. Cook over moderate heat until the poultry and onion pieces are lightly browned, stirring from time to time so they colour evenly.

3 Add the remaining ingredients. Partially cover the stockpot and gently simmer the stock for about 3 hours.

5 When cold, carefully remove the layer of fat that will have set on the surface.

2 Add the water and stir well to mix in the sediment on the bottom of the pot. Bring to the boil and skim off the impurities as they rise to the surface of the stock.

4 Strain the stock into a bowl and leave to cool, then refrigerate.

FRUGAL STOCK

Stock can be made from the bones and carcasses of roasted poultry, cooked with vegetables and flavourings. Save the carcasses in a plastic bag in the freezer until you have three or four, then make stock. It may not have quite as rich a flavour as stock made from a whole bird or fresh wings, backs and necks, but it will still taste fresher and less salty than stock made from a commercial cube.

STOCK TIPS

If wished, use a whole bird for making stock instead of wings, backs and necks. A boiling fowl, if available, will give wonderful flavour and provide meat to use in salads, sandwiches, soups and casseroles.

No salt is added to stock because as the stock reduces, the flavour becomes concentrated and saltiness increases. Add salt to dishes which contain the stock.

Making Poultry Sautés

*A sauté combines frying and brais-
ing, producing particularly
succulent results. It is a method
suitable for pieces of poultry as well
as for small whole birds such as
quails and poussins.*

*As with frying, the poultry should
be dried thoroughly with kitchen
paper before cooking, to ensure that
it browns quickly and evenly.*

1 Heat a little oil, a mixture of oil
and butter, or clarified butter
in a heavy frying pan or sauté pan.

2 Add the poultry and fry over
moderate heat until it is golden
brown, turning to colour evenly.

3 Add any liquid and flavourings
called for in the recipe. Bring
to the boil, then cover and reduce
the heat to moderately low.
Continue cooking gently until the
poultry is done, turning the pieces
or birds over once or twice.

4 If the recipe instructs, remove
the poultry from the pan and
keep it warm while finishing the
sauce. This can be as simple as
boiling the cooking juices to
reduce them or adding butter or
cream for a richer result.

5 To thicken the cooking juices
use equal weights of butter and
flour mashed together. Use 25g/
1oz of this "beurre manié" to
250ml/8fl oz/1 cup liquid. Add
small pieces gradually to the hot
juices and whisk until smooth.

6 Another method of thickening
cooking juices is to use
cornflour. Blend 10ml/2 tsp
cornflour with 15ml/1 tbsp water
and add to 250ml/8fl oz/1 cup
juices. Boil, whisking, for 2–3
minutes, until the sauce is syrupy.

COUNTRY CHICKEN SAUTE
~

Cook 175g/6oz chopped bacon
in 10ml/2 tsp oil over a
moderately high heat until
lightly coloured. Remove and
reserve. Dredge a 1.5kg/3¹/₂lb
chicken, cut into eight pieces, in
seasoned flour. Fry in the bacon
fat until evenly browned. Add
45ml/3 tbsp dry white wine and
250ml/8fl oz/1 cup poultry
stock. Bring to the boil and add
225g/8oz quartered mushrooms
sautéed in 15ml/1 tbsp of butter
and the reserved bacon. Cover
and cook over low heat for
20–25 minutes, or until the
chicken is tender.
Serves 4.

Frying Chicken

*Fried chicken is justifiably popular –
crisp and brown outside and tender
and juicy within. It's a quick and
easy cooking method that can be
applied to pieces of rabbit and hare
and small turkey joints, too.*

*Dry the pieces thoroughly with
kitchen paper before frying. If they
are at all wet, they will not brown
properly. If the recipe directs, lightly
coat the pieces with egg and crumbs
or with a batter.*

1 To pan-fry, heat oil, a mixture
of oil and butter, or clarified
butter in a large, heavy-based
frying pan over moderate heat.
When very hot, add the chicken
pieces, skin-side down.

2 Fry until deep golden brown all
over, turning the pieces during
cooking. Fry until the pieces are
thoroughly cooked. Remove pieces
of breast before drumsticks and
thighs. Drain on kitchen paper.

SUCCULENT FRIED CHICKEN
～

Mix 250ml/8fl oz/1 cup milk
with 1 beaten egg in a shallow
dish. On a sheet of greaseproof
paper combine 150g/5oz/1¹/₄
cups plain flour, 5ml/1 tsp
paprika, and some salt and
pepper. One at a time, dip eight
chicken pieces in the egg mixture
and turn them to coat all over.
Then dip in the seasoned flour
and shake off any excess. Deep-
fry for 25–30 minutes, turning
the pieces so they brown and
cook evenly. Drain on kitchen
paper and serve very hot.
Serves 4.

3 To deep-fry, dip the pieces into
a mixture of milk and beaten
egg and coat lightly with seasoned
flour. Allow coating to set for
20 minutes before frying. (Or dip
them in batter just before frying.)

4 Half fill a deep pan with
vegetable oil. Heat it to 185°C/
365°F. You can test the temperature
with a cube of bread; if it takes
50 seconds to brown, the oil is at
the right temperature.

5 With a fish slice or tongs, lower
the chicken pieces into the oil,
a few at a time. Deep-fry, turning
during cooking, until they are
golden brown all over and cooked.

6 Drain on kitchen paper and
serve hot. If you want to keep a
batch of fried chicken hot whilst
frying the rest, put it, uncovered,
into a low oven.

Poaching, Casseroling & Braising

SIMPLE CHICKEN STOCK

This all-purpose chicken stock may be used as the basis for a wonderful home-made soup.

1 Put the giblets (the neck, gizzard and heart, but not the liver, as this makes stock bitter), or the carcass from a cooked chicken, into a pan and just cover with cold water.

2 Add a quartered onion, carrot, bouquet garni (bay leaf, thyme and parsley) and a few pepper-corns. Bring to the boil, cover and simmer gently for 1–2 hours.

3 Remove any scum that rises to the surface with a slotted draining spoon. Alternatively, make the stock when you cook the chicken, by putting the giblets in the roasting tin around the chicken with the onion and herbs and just enough water to stop them from burning.

4 When the stock has set, care-fully remove the fat from the surface with a spoon. Add salt to taste when using the stock.

POACHING

Poaching is a very gentle cooking method and produces stock for making a sauce afterwards.

1 Put the chicken into a flame-proof casserole with a bouquet garni (bay leaf, thyme and parsley), carrot and onion.

2 Cover with water and add salt and peppercorns. Bring to the boil, cover and simmer for about 1¹⁄₂ hours or until tender.

3 Cool in the liquid or lift out, shred, and combine with a white sauce.

BRAISING

This method can be used for whole chickens and pieces and is ideal for strongly-flavoured meat.

1 Heat olive oil in a flameproof casserole and lightly fry a chicken or joints until golden.

2 Remove the chicken and fry 450g/1lb of diced vegetables (carrots, onions, celery and turnips), until soft.

3 Replace the chicken, cover tightly and cook very slowly on the hob or in a preheated oven at 160°C/325°F/Gas 3, until tender.

CASSEROLING

This slow-cooking method is good for large chicken joints with bones, or more mature meat.

1 Heat olive oil in a flameproof casserole and brown the chicken joints.

2 Add some stock, wine or a mixture of both to a depth of 2.5cm/1in. Add seasonings and herbs, cover, and cook on the hob or in the oven as for braising for 1–1¹⁄₂ hours or until tender.

3 Add a selection of lightly-fried vegetables such as baby onions, mushrooms, carrots and small new potatoes about halfway through the cooking time.

Five Stuffings for Chicken

BASIC HERB STUFFING

INGREDIENTS

1 small onion, finely chopped
15g/^{1}/2oz/1 tbsp butter
115g/4oz/2 cups fresh breadcrumbs
15ml/1 tbsp chopped fresh parsley
5ml/1 tsp mixed dried herbs
1 egg, beaten
salt and black pepper

Cook the onion gently in the butter until tender. Allow to cool.

Add to the remaining ingredients and then mix thoroughly. Season well with salt and pepper.

VARIATIONS

Any of these ingredients may be added to the basic recipe to vary the flavour of the stuffing, depending on what you have in your store cupboard at home.

1 celery stick, finely chopped
1 small eating apple, diced
50g/2oz/^{1}/2 cup chopped walnuts or
    almonds
25g/1oz/1 tbsp raisins or sultanas
50g/2oz/^{1}/4 cup chopped dried prunes or
    apricots
50g/2oz mushrooms, finely chopped
grated rind of ^{1}/2 orange or lemon
50g/2oz/^{1}/2 cup pine nuts
2 rashers streaky bacon, chopped

APRICOT AND ORANGE STUFFING

INGREDIENTS

1 small onion, finely chopped
15g/^{1}/2 oz/1 tbsp butter
115g/4oz/2 cups fresh breadcrumbs
50g/2oz/^{1}/4 cup finely chopped dried
    apricots
grated rind of ^{1}/2 orange
1 small egg, beaten
15ml/1 tbsp chopped fresh parsley
salt and black pepper

Heat the butter in a frying pan and cook the onion gently until tender.

Allow to cool slightly, and add to the rest of the ingredients. Mix until thoroughly combined and season with salt and pepper.

RAISIN AND NUT STUFFING

INGREDIENTS

115g/4oz/2 cups fresh breadcrumbs
50g/2oz/^{1}/3 cup raisins
50g/2oz/^{1}/2 cup walnuts, almonds, pistachios or pine nuts
15ml/1 tbsp chopped fresh parsley
5ml/1 tsp chopped mixed herbs
1 small egg, beaten
25g/1oz/2 tbsp melted butter
salt and black pepper

Mix all the ingredients together thoroughly. Season well with salt and pepper.

Raisin and Nut Stuffing

PARSLEY, LEMON AND THYME STUFFING

INGREDIENTS

115g/4oz/2 cups fresh breadcrumbs
25g/1oz/2 tbsp butter
15ml/1 tbsp chopped fresh parsley
2.5ml/^{1}/2 tsp dried thyme
grated rind of ^{1}/4 lemon
1 rasher streaky bacon, chopped
1 small egg, beaten
salt and black pepper

Mix all the ingredients together to combine them thoroughly.

Parsley, Lemon and Thyme Stuffing

SAUSAGEMEAT STUFFING

INGREDIENTS

15g/^{1}/2 oz/1 tbsp butter
1 small onion, finely chopped
2 rashers streaky bacon, chopped
225g/8oz sausagemeat
2.5ml/^{1}/2 tsp mixed dried herbs
salt and black pepper

Heat the butter in a frying pan and cook the onion until tender. Add the bacon and cook for 5 minutes, then allow to cool.

Add to the remaining ingredients and mix thoroughly.

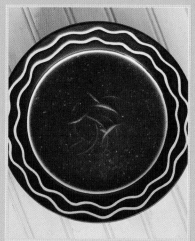
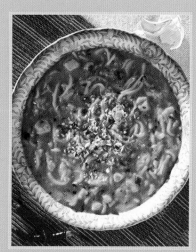

SOUPS
& STARTERS

~

Chicken and Lentil Soup

A chunky soup which will make a good lunchtime dish.

Serves 4

25g/1oz/2 tbsp butter or margarine
1 large carrot, chopped
1 onion, chopped
1 leek, white part only, chopped
1 celery stick, chopped
115g/4oz mushrooms, chopped
45ml/3 tbsp dry white wine
1 litre/1³/4 pints/4 cups chicken stock
10ml/2 tsp dried thyme
1 bay leaf
115g/4oz/¹/2 cup brown or green lentils
225g/8oz cooked chicken, diced
salt and black pepper

1 Melt the butter or margarine in a large saucepan. Add the carrot, onion, leek, celery and mushrooms. Cook for 3–5 minutes, until softened.

2 Stir in the wine and chicken stock. Bring to the boil and skim off any foam that rises to the surface. Add the thyme and bay leaf. Reduce the heat, cover, and simmer for 30 minutes.

3 Add the lentils and continue cooking, covered, for another 30–40 minutes, until they are just tender, stirring the soup from time to time.

4 Stir in the diced chicken and season to taste with salt and pepper. Cook until just heated through. Ladle the soup into bowls and serve hot.

Chicken Vermicelli Soup with Egg Shreds

This light soup can be put together in a matter of moments and is full of flavour.

INGREDIENTS

Serves 4–6

3 size 1 eggs

30ml/2 tbsp chopped fresh coriander or
  parsley

1.5 litres/2^1/2 pints/6^1/4 cups good
  chicken stock or canned consommé

115g/4oz/1 cup dried vermicelli or angel
  hair pasta

115g/4oz cooked chicken breast, sliced

salt and pepper

1 First make the egg shreds.
Whisk the eggs together in a
small bowl and stir in the chopped
coriander or parsley.

2 Heat a small non-stick frying
pan and pour in 30–45ml/
2–3 tbsp egg, swirling to cover the
base evenly. Cook until set. Repeat
until all the mixture is used up.

3 Roll each pancake up and slice
thinly into shreds. Set aside.

4 Bring the stock to the boil and
add the pasta, breaking it into
short lengths. Cook for 3–5
minutes until the pasta is almost
tender, then add the chicken, salt
and pepper. Heat through for 2–3
minutes, then stir in the egg
shreds. Serve immediately.

Cream of Spring Onion Soup

A meltingly smooth soup of chicken stock, potato and spring onions.

Serves 4–6

25g/1oz/2 tbsp butter

1 small onion, chopped

150g/5oz spring onions, white parts only, chopped

225g/8oz potato, peeled and chopped

600ml/1 pint/2$^{1}/_{2}$ cups chicken stock

350ml/12fl oz/1$^{1}/_{2}$ cups single cream

salt and white pepper

30ml/2 tbsp lemon juice

chopped spring onion greens or fresh chives, to garnish

1 Melt the butter in a saucepan and add all the onions. Cover and cook over very low heat for about 10 minutes or until soft.

2 Add the potatoes and the stock. Bring to the boil, cover again and simmer over a moderately low heat for 30 minutes. Cool slightly.

3 Purée the soup in a blender or in a food processor.

4 If serving the soup hot, pour it back into the pan. Add the cream and season. Reheat gently, stirring frequently. Stir in the lemon juice and garnish before serving.

Courgette Soup with Small Pasta Shells

An attractive and refreshing soup which could be made using cucumber instead of courgettes.

Serves 4–6

60ml/4 tbsp olive or sunflower oil

2 medium onions, finely chopped

1.5 litres/2^1/2 pints/6^1/4 cups chicken
    stock

900g/2lb courgettes

115g/4oz/1 cup small pasta for soup

fresh lemon juice

salt and pepper

30ml/2 tbsp chopped fresh chervil

soured cream, to serve

1 Heat the oil in a large saucepan and add the onions. Cover and cook gently for about 20 minutes until very soft but not coloured, stirring occasionally.

2 Add the chicken stock and bring to the boil.

3 Meanwhile grate the courgettes and stir into the boiling stock with the pasta. Turn down the heat and simmer for 15 minutes until the pasta is tender. Season to taste with lemon juice, salt and pepper.

4 Stir in the chervil and add a swirl of soured cream to serve.

Country Vegetable Soup

To ring the changes, vary the
vegetables according to the season.

INGREDIENTS

Serves 4

50g/2oz/4 tbsp butter

1 onion, chopped

2 leeks, sliced

2 celery sticks, sliced

2 carrots, sliced

2 small turnips, chopped

4 ripe tomatoes, skinned and chopped

1 litre/1^{3}/4 pints/4 cups chicken stock

bouquet garni

115g/4oz green beans, chopped

salt and pepper

chopped herbs such as tarragon, thyme,
    chives and parsley, to garnish

1 Heat the butter in a large
saucepan, add the onion and
leeks and cook gently until soft but
not coloured.

2 Add the celery, carrots and
turnips and cook for 3–4
minutes, stirring occasionally. Stir
in the tomatoes and stock, add the
bouquet garni and simmer for
about 20 minutes.

3 Add the beans to the soup and
cook until all the vegetables are
tender. Season to taste and serve
garnished with chopped herbs.

Split Pea and Bacon Soup

Another name for this soup is
"London Particular", from the dense
fogs for which the city used to be
notorious. The fogs in turn were
named "pea-soupers".

INGREDIENTS

Serves 4

15g/^{1}/2 oz/1 tbsp butter

115g/4oz smoked back bacon, chopped

1 large onion, chopped

1 carrot, chopped

1 celery stick, chopped

75g/3oz/scant ^{1}/2 cup split peas

1.2 litres/2 pints/5 cups chicken stock

2 thick slices firm bread, buttered and
    without crusts

2 slices streaky bacon

salt and pepper

1 Heat the butter in a saucepan,
add the smoked back bacon
and cook until the fat runs. Stir in
the onion, carrot and celery and
cook for 2–3 minutes.

2 Add the split peas followed by
the stock. Bring to the boil,
stirring occasionally, then cover
and simmer for 45–60 minutes.

3 Meanwhile, preheat the oven
to 180°C/350°F/Gas 4 and bake
the bread, on a baking sheet, for
about 20 minutes, until crisp and
brown, then cut into cubes.

4 Grill the streaky bacon until
very crisp, then chop finely.

5 When the soup is ready, season
to taste and serve hot with
chopped bacon and croûtons
scattered on each portion.

Mulligatawny Soup

Mulligatawny (which means "pepper water") was introduced into England in the late eighteenth century, by members of the army and colonial service returning home from India.

INGREDIENTS

Serves 4

50g/2oz/4 tbsp butter or 60ml/4 tbsp oil
2 large chicken joints, about
   350g/12oz each
1 onion, chopped
1 carrot, chopped
1 small turnip, chopped
about 15ml/1 tbsp curry powder, to taste
4 cloves
6 black peppercorns, lightly crushed
50g/2oz/^{1}/4 cup lentils
900ml/1^{1}/2 pints/3^{3}/4 cups chicken stock
40g/1^{1}/2 oz/^{1}/4 cup sultanas
salt and pepper

1 Melt the butter or heat the oil in a large saucepan and brown the chicken over a brisk heat. Transfer the chicken on to a plate.

2 Add the onion, carrot and turnip to the pan and cook, stirring occasionally, until lightly coloured. Stir in the curry powder, cloves and peppercorns and cook for 1–2 minutes. Add the lentils.

COOK'S TIP

Red split lentils will give the best colour for this dish, although green or brown lentils could be used if you prefer.

3 Pour in the stock and bring to the boil. Add the sultanas and chicken and any juices from the plate. Cover and simmer gently for about 1^{1}/4 hours.

4 Remove the chicken from the pan and discard the skin and bones. Chop the flesh, return to the soup and reheat. Check and adjust the seasoning before serving the soup piping hot.

Thai Chicken Soup

This filling and tasty soup is very quick to prepare and cook.

INGREDIENTS

Serves 4

15ml/1 tbsp vegetable oil

1 garlic clove, finely chopped

2 boned chicken breasts, about 175g/6oz
   each, skinned and chopped

2.5ml/^{1}/$_2$ tsp ground turmeric

1.5ml/^{1}/$_4$ tsp hot chilli powder

75g/3oz creamed coconut

900ml/1^1/$_2$ pints/3^3/$_4$ cups hot
   chicken stock

30ml/2 tbsp lemon or lime juice

30ml/2 tbsp crunchy peanut butter

50g/2oz/1 cup thread egg noodles, broken
   into small pieces

15ml/1 tbsp spring onions, finely chopped

15ml/1 tbsp chopped fresh coriander

salt and black pepper

30ml/2 tbsp desiccated coconut and ^{1}/$_2$
   fresh red chilli, seeded and finely
   chopped, to garnish

1 Heat the oil in a large pan and fry the garlic for 1 minute until lightly golden. Add the chicken and spices and stir-fry for a further 3–4 minutes.

2 Crumble the creamed coconut into the hot chicken stock and stir until dissolved. Pour on to the chicken and add the lemon juice, peanut butter and egg noodles.

3 Cover the pan and simmer for about 15 minutes.

4 Add the spring onions and fresh coriander, then season well and cook for a further 5 minutes. Meanwhile, place the desiccated coconut and chilli in a small frying pan and heat for 2–3 minutes, stirring frequently.

5 Serve the soup in bowls and sprinkle each one with some fried coconut and chilli.

New England Spiced Pumpkin Soup

*Pumpkin soup cooked with spices,
brown sugar and orange juice.*

Serves 4

25g/1oz/2 tbsp butter
1 onion, finely chopped
1 small garlic clove, crushed
15ml/1 tbsp plain flour
pinch of grated nutmeg
2.5ml/^{1}/$_2$ tsp ground cinnamon
350g/12oz/3 cups pumpkin, seeded,
    peeled and cubed
600ml/1 pint/2^1/$_2$ cups chicken stock
150ml/^{1}/$_4$ pint/^{2}/$_3$ cup orange juice
5ml/1 tsp brown sugar
15ml/1 tbsp vegetable oil
2 slices Granary bread without crusts
30ml/2 tbsp sunflower seeds
salt and black pepper

1 Heat the butter in a large saucepan, add the onion and garlic and fry gently for 4–5 minutes, until softened. Stir in the flour, all the spices and the pumpkin.

2 Cover and cook gently for about 6 minutes, stirring occasionally.

3 Pour in the chicken stock and orange juice and add the brown sugar. Cover and bring to the boil, then reduce the heat and simmer for 20 minutes, until the pumpkin has softened.

4 Pour half of the mixture into a blender or food processor and process until smooth. Return the soup to the pan with the remaining chunky mixture. Season well and heat through, stirring.

5 Meanwhile, make the croûtons. Heat the oil in a frying pan, cut the bread into cubes and fry gently until just beginning to brown. Add the sunflower seeds and fry for 1–2 minutes. Drain the croûtons and sunflower seeds on kitchen paper.

6 Serve the soup hot with a few of the croûtons and sunflower seeds scattered over the top. Serve the rest separately.

Green Pea and Mint Soup

This soup is equally delicious cold.
Instead of reheating it after
puréeing, leave it to cool and then
chill lightly in the fridge. Stir in the
swirl of cream just before serving.

INGREDIENTS

Serves 4

50g/2oz/4 tbsp butter

4 spring onions, chopped

450g/1lb/4 cups fresh or frozen peas

600ml/1 pint/2^1/$_2$ cups chicken
    stock

2 large mint sprigs

600ml/1 pint/2^1/$_2$ cups milk

pinch of sugar (optional)

salt and pepper

single cream, to serve

small mint sprigs, to garnish

1 Heat the butter in a large
saucepan, add the spring
onions, and cook gently until
softened but not coloured.

**FREEZER
NOTE**

The soup can be frozen for up to
two months after step 2. Allow it
to thaw in the fridge before
puréeing and reheating.

---

2 Stir the peas into the pan, add
the stock and mint and bring
to the boil. Cover and simmer very
gently for about 30 minutes for
fresh peas or 15 minutes if you are
using frozen peas, until the peas
are very tender. Remove about
45ml/3 tbsp of the peas using a
slotted spoon, and put to one side
for the garnish.

3 Pour the soup into a food
processor or blender, add the
milk and purée until smooth.
Then return the soup to the pan
and reheat gently. Season to taste,
adding a pinch of sugar, if liked.

4 Pour the soup into individual
bowls. Swirl a little cream into
each, then garnish with mint and
the reserved peas.

Carrot and Coriander Soup

Use a good home-made stock for this soup – it adds a far greater depth of flavour than stock made from cubes.

Serves 4

50g/2oz/4 tbsp butter

3 leeks, sliced

450g/1lb carrots, sliced

15ml/1 tbsp ground coriander

1.2 litres/2 pints/5 cups chicken stock

150ml/1/4 pint/2/3 cup Greek-style yogurt

salt and black pepper

30–45ml/2–3 tbsp chopped fresh coriander, to garnish

1 Melt the butter in a large pan. Add the leeks and carrots and stir well to coat with the butter. Cover and cook for about 10 minutes, until the vegetables are beginning to soften but not colour.

2 Stir in the ground coriander and cook for about 1 minute. Pour in the stock and season to taste. Bring to the boil, cover and simmer for about 20 minutes, until the leeks and carrots are tender.

3 Leave to cool slightly, then purée the soup in a blender until smooth. Return the soup to the pan and add 30ml/2 tbsp of the yogurt, then taste the soup and adjust the seasoning. Reheat gently but do not boil.

4 Ladle the soup into bowls and add a spoonful of yogurt to the centre of each. Scatter over the coriander and serve immediately.

Leek, Potato and Rocket Soup

Rocket, with its distinctive, peppery taste, is wonderful in this deliciously filling soup. Serve it hot with ciabatta croûtons.

Serves 4–6

50g/2oz/4 tbsp butter

1 onion, chopped

3 leeks, chopped

2 potatoes, diced

900ml/1¹/2 pints/3³/4 cups light
    chicken stock

2 large handfuls rocket, roughly
    chopped

150ml/¹/4 pint/²/3 cup double cream

salt and black pepper

garlic-flavoured croûtons, to serve

1 Melt the butter in a large heavy-based pan, add the onion, leeks and potatoes and stir until the vegetables are coated.

2 Cover and leave the vegetables to sweat for about 15 minutes. Pour in the stock, cover once again, then simmer the vegetables for 20 minutes, until tender.

3 Press the soup through a sieve or food mill and return to the rinsed-out pan. (When puréeing the soup, don't use a blender or food processor, as these will give the soup a gluey texture.) Add the chopped rocket and cook gently for 5 minutes.

4 Stir in the cream, then season to taste and reheat gently. Ladle the soup into warm soup bowls and serve with the garlic-flavoured croûtons.

Split Pea and Courgette Soup

*Rich and satisfying, this tasty and
nutritious soup will warm you up
on a chilly winter's day.*

INGREDIENTS

Serves 4

175g/6oz/1 cup yellow split peas
1 medium onion, finely chopped
5ml/1 tsp sunflower oil
2 medium courgettes, finely diced
900ml/1 1/2 pints/3 3/4 cups chicken stock
2.5ml/1/2 tsp ground turmeric
salt and black pepper

3 Reserve a handful of courgettes
and add the rest to the pan.
Cook, stirring, for 2–3 minutes.
Add the stock and turmeric and
bring to the boil. Reduce the heat,
then cover and simmer for 30–40
minutes, or until the peas are tender.

4 When the soup is almost ready,
bring a saucepan of water to
the boil, add the reserved diced
courgettes and cook for 1 minute,
then drain and add to the soup.
Adjust the seasoning to taste.

1 Place the split peas in a bowl,
cover with cold water and leave
to soak for several hours or
overnight. Drain, rinse in cold
water and drain again.

2 Cook the onion in the oil in a
covered pan, shaking the pan
occasionally, until soft.

COOK'S TIP

For a quicker alternative, use
split red lentils for this soup –
they need no presoaking and
cook very quickly. Adjust the
amount of stock, if necessary.

Red Pepper Soup with Lime

The beautiful rich red colour of this soup makes it a very attractive starter or light lunch. For a special dinner, toast some tiny croûtons and serve sprinkled on to the soup.

INGREDIENTS

Serves 4–6

4 red peppers, seeded and chopped

1 large onion, chopped

5ml/1 tsp olive oil

1 garlic clove, crushed

1 small red chilli, sliced

45ml/3 tbsp tomato purée

900ml/$1^1/_2$ pints/$3^3/_4$ cups chicken stock

finely grated rind and juice of 1 lime

salt and black pepper

shreds of lime rind, to garnish

1 Cook the chopped peppers and onion gently in the oil in a covered saucepan for about 5 minutes until softened, shaking the pan occasionally.

2 Stir in the garlic, then add the chilli with the tomato purée. Stir in half the stock, then bring to the boil. Cover the pan and simmer for 10 minutes.

3 Cool slightly, then purée in a food processor or blender. Return to the pan, then add the remaining stock, the lime rind and juice, and seasoning.

4 Bring the soup back to the boil, then serve at once with a few strips of lime rind, scattered into each bowl.

Jerusalem Artichoke Soup

Topped with saffron cream, this
soup is wonderful on a wintry day.

INGREDIENTS

Serves 4

50g/2oz/4 tbsp butter

1 onion, chopped

450g/1lb Jerusalem artichokes, peeled and
   cut into chunks

900ml/1¹/2 pints/3³/4 cups chicken stock

150ml/¹/4 pint/²/3 cup milk

150ml/¹/4 pint/²/3 cup double cream

good pinch of saffron powder

salt and black pepper

snipped fresh chives, to garnish

1 Melt the butter in a large
heavy-based pan and cook
the chopped onion for about
5–8 minutes, until soft but not
browned, stirring occasionally.

2 Add the artichokes to the pan
and stir until coated in the
butter. Cover and cook gently for
10–15 minutes; do not allow the
artichokes to brown. Pour in the
stock and milk, then cover and
simmer for 15 minutes. Cool
slightly, then process in a blender
or food processor until smooth.

3 Strain the soup back into the
pan. Add half the cream,
season to taste and reheat gently.
Lightly whip the remaining cream
with the saffron powder. Ladle the
soup into warmed soup bowls and
put a spoonful of saffron cream in
the centre of each. Scatter over the
snipped chives and serve at once.

Broccoli and Stilton Soup

A really easy, but rich, soup – choose
something simple to follow, such as
plainly roasted or grilled meat,
poultry or fish.

INGREDIENTS

Serves 4

350g/12oz broccoli

25g/1oz/2 tbsp butter

1 onion, chopped

1 leek, white part only, chopped

1 small potato, cut into chunks

600ml/1 pint/2¹/2 cups hot chicken stock

300ml/¹/2 pint/1¹/4 cups milk

45ml/3 tbsp double cream

115g/4oz Stilton cheese, rind removed,
   crumbled

salt and black pepper

1 Break the broccoli into florets,
discarding any tough stems. Set
aside two small, well-shaped florets
to use for the garnish.

2 Melt the butter in a large pan
and cook the onion and leek
until soft but not coloured. Add
the broccoli and potato, then pour
in the stock. Cover and simmer for
15–20 minutes, until tender.

3 Cool slightly, then purée the
soup in a blender or food
processor. Strain through a sieve
back into the pan.

4 Add the milk, cream and
seasoning to the pan and
reheat gently. At the last minute
add the cheese, stirring until it just
melts. Do not boil.

5 Meanwhile, blanch the
reserved broccoli florets and
cut them vertically into thin slices.
Ladle the soup into warm bowls
and garnish with the broccoli and
freshly ground black pepper.

Beetroot and Apricot Swirl

This soup is most attractive if you swirl together the two coloured mixtures, but if you prefer they can be mixed together to save on time and washing up.

INGREDIENTS

Serves 4

4 large cooked beetroot, roughly
   chopped
1 small onion, roughly chopped
600ml/1 pint/2^{1}/$_{2}$ cups chicken stock
200g/7oz/1 cup ready-to-eat
   dried apricots
250ml/8fl oz/1 cup orange juice
salt and black pepper

1 Place the beetroot and half the onion in a pan with the stock. Bring to the boil, then reduce the heat, cover and simmer for about 10 minutes. Purée in a food processor or blender.

2 Place the rest of the onion in a saucepan with the apricots and orange juice, cover and simmer gently for about 15 minutes, until tender. Process to a purée in a food processor or blender.

3 Return the two mixtures to the saucepans and reheat. Season to taste with salt and pepper, then swirl them together in individual soup bowls for a marbled effect.

COOK'S TIP

The apricot mixture should be the same consistency as the beetroot mixture – if it is too thick, then add a little more orange juice.

Spicy Sweetcorn Soup

This is a very quick and easy soup, made in minutes. If you are using frozen prawns, then defrost them first before adding to the soup.

INGREDIENTS

Serves 4

2.5ml/$\frac{1}{2}$ tsp sesame or sunflower oil

2 spring onions, thinly sliced

1 garlic clove, crushed

600ml/1 pint/2$\frac{1}{2}$ cups chicken stock

425g/15oz can cream-style sweetcorn

225g/8oz/1$\frac{1}{4}$ cups cooked, peeled prawns

5ml/1 tsp green chilli paste or
    chilli sauce (optional)

salt and black pepper

fresh coriander leaves, to garnish

1 Heat the oil in a large heavy-based saucepan and sauté the spring onions and garlic over a medium heat for 1 minute, until softened, but not browned.

COOK'S TIP

If cream-style corn is not available, use ordinary canned sweetcorn, puréed in a food processor for just a few seconds, until creamy yet with some texture left.

2 Stir in the chicken stock, cream-style sweetcorn, prawns and chilli paste or sauce, if using.

3 Bring the soup to the boil, stirring occasionally. Season to taste, then serve at once, sprinkled with fresh coriander leaves.

Chicken Goujons

Serve as a first course for eight people or as a filling main course for four. Delicious served with new baby potatoes and a green salad.

INGREDIENTS

Serves 8

4 boned and skinned chicken breasts
175g/6oz/3 cups fresh breadcrumbs
5ml/1 tsp ground coriander
10ml/2 tsp ground paprika
2.5ml/^{1}/2 tsp ground cumin
45ml/3 tbsp plain flour
2 eggs, beaten
oil, for deep-frying
salt and black pepper
lemon slices, to garnish
sprigs of fresh coriander, to garnish

For the dip

300ml/^{1}/2 pint/1^1/4 cups Greek yogurt
30ml/2 tbsp lemon juice
60ml/4 tbsp chopped fresh coriander
60ml/4 tbsp chopped fresh parsley

1 Divide the chicken breasts into two natural fillets. Place them between two sheets of clear film and using a rolling pin, flatten each one to a thickness of 1cm/^{1}/2 in.

2 Cut the chicken into diagonal 2.5cm/1in strips.

3 Mix the breadcrumbs with the spices and seasoning. Toss the chicken fillet pieces (goujons) into the flour, keeping them separate.

4 Dip the goujons into the beaten egg and then coat in the breadcrumb mixture.

5 Thoroughly mix all the ingredients for the dip together and season to taste. Cover and chill until required.

6 Heat the oil in a heavy-based pan. It is ready for deep-frying when a piece of bread tossed into the oil sizzles on the surface. Fry the goujons in batches until golden and crisp. Drain on kitchen paper and keep warm in the oven until all the chicken has been fried. Garnish with lemon slices and sprigs of fresh coriander and serve with the yogurt dip.

Corn-fed Chicken Salad

*A light first course for eight or a
substantial main course for four.*

INGREDIENTS

Serves 8

1.75kg/4lb corn-fed chicken

300ml/^{1}/$_2$ pint/1^1/$_4$ cups white wine
 and water, mixed

24 x 5mm/^{1}/$_4$ in slices French bread

1 garlic clove, peeled

225g/8oz French beans, trimmed and cut
 in 5cm/2in lengths

115g/4oz fresh young spinach leaves,
 washed and torn into small pieces

2 sticks celery, thinly sliced

2 sun-dried tomatoes, chopped

2 spring onions, thinly sliced

fresh chives and parsley, to garnish

For the vinaigrette

30ml/2 tbsp red wine vinegar

90ml/6 tbsp olive oil

15ml/1 tbsp wholegrain mustard

15ml/1 tbsp clear honey

30ml/2 tbsp chopped mixed fresh herbs

10ml/2 tsp finely chopped capers

salt and black pepper

2 Put all the ingredients for the
vinaigrette into a screw-topped
jar and shake vigorously. Adjust
the seasoning to taste.

3 Toast the French bread until
golden brown. Rub with garlic.

4 Cook the French beans in
boiling water until just tender.
Drain and rinse under cold water.

5 Arrange the spinach on serving
plates with the celery, French
beans, sun-dried tomatoes,
chicken and spring onions. Spoon
over the dressing, add the toasted
croûtes and garnish with chives
and parsley.

1 Preheat the oven to 190°C/
375°F/Gas 5. Put the chicken,
wine and water into a casserole.
Roast for 1^1/$_2$ hours until tender.
Leave to cool in the liquid. Remove
the skin and bones and cut the
flesh into small pieces.

Chicken Liver Pâté

A deliciously smooth pâté which is ideal to spread on hot toast.

Serves 6 or more
50g/2oz/4 tbsp butter
1 onion, finely chopped
350g/12oz chicken livers, trimmed of all
    dark or greenish parts
60ml/4 tbsp medium sherry
25g/1oz full-fat soft cheese
15–30ml/1–2 tbsp lemon juice
2 hard-boiled eggs, chopped
salt and pepper
50–75g/2–3oz/¹⁄₄ cup clarified butter

1 Melt the butter in a frying pan. Add the onion and livers and cook until the onion is soft and the livers are lightly browned and no longer pink in the centre.

2 Add the sherry and boil until reduced by half. Cool slightly.

> COOK'S TIP
>
> Add brandy instead of sherry for a special occasion dinner party.

3 Turn the mixture into a food processor or blender and add the soft cheese and 1 tablespoon lemon juice. Blend until smooth.

4 Add the hard-boiled eggs and blend briefly. Season with salt and pepper. Taste and add more lemon juice if liked.

5 Pack the liver pâté into a mould or into individual ramekins. Smooth the surface.

6 Spoon a layer of clarified butter over the surface of the pâté. Chill until firm. Serve at room temperature, with hot toast or savoury biscuits.

Chicken and Avocado Mayonnaise

You need quite firm scoops or forks to eat this starter, so don't be tempted to try to pass it round as a finger food.

Serves 4

30ml/2 tbsp mayonnaise

15ml/1 tbsp fromage frais

2 garlic cloves, crushed

115g/4oz/1 cup chopped cooked chicken

1 large ripe, but firm, avocado,
    peeled and stoned

30ml/2 tbsp lemon juice

salt and black pepper

nacho chips or tortilla chips, to serve

1 Mix together the mayonnaise, fromage frais, garlic, and seasoning to taste, in a small bowl. Stir in the chopped chicken.

COOK'S TIP

This mixture also makes a great, chunky filling for sandwiches, baps or pitta bread. Or serve as a main course salad, heaped on to a base of mixed salad leaves.

2 Chop the avocado and toss immediately in lemon juice.

3 Mix the avocado gently into the chicken mixture. Check the seasoning and chill until required.

4 Serve in small serving dishes with the nacho or tortilla chips as scoops, if liked.

Nutty Chicken Balls

Serve these as a first course with the lemon sauce, or make them into smaller balls and serve on cocktail sticks as canapés.

INGREDIENTS

Serves 4

350g/12oz chicken

50g/2oz/^{1}/$_2$ cup pistachio nuts, finely chopped

15ml/1 tbsp lemon juice

2 eggs, beaten

plain flour, for shaping

75g/3oz/1^1/$_4$ cups blanched chopped almonds

75g/3oz/^{3}/$_4$ cup dried breadcrumbs

salt and black pepper

For the lemon sauce

150ml/^{1}/$_4$ pint/^{2}/$_3$ cup chicken stock

225g/8oz/1 cup cream cheese

15ml/1 tbsp lemon juice

15ml/1 tbsp chopped fresh parsley

15ml/1 tbsp snipped fresh chives

1 Skin and mince or chop the chicken finely. Mix with salt and freshly ground black pepper, pistachio nuts, lemon juice and one beaten egg.

2 Shape into sixteen small balls with floured hands (use a spoon as a guide, so that all the balls are roughly the same size). Roll the balls in the remaining beaten egg and coat firstly with the almonds and then the dried breadcrumbs, pressing on firmly. Chill until ready to cook.

3 Preheat the oven to 190°C/375°F/Gas 5. Place the balls on a greased baking sheet and bake for about 15 minutes or until golden brown and crisp.

4 To make the lemon sauce, gently heat the chicken stock and cream cheese together in a pan, whisking until smooth. Add the lemon juice, herbs and seasoning. Serve with the chicken balls.

Spiced Chicken Livers

Chicken livers can be bought frozen, but make sure that you defrost them thoroughly before using. Serve as a first course or light meal along with a mixed salad and garlic bread.

Serves 4

350g/12oz chicken livers
115g/4oz/1 cup plain flour
2.5ml/^{1}/$_2$ tsp ground coriander
2.5ml/^{1}/$_2$ tsp ground cumin
2.5ml/^{1}/$_2$ tsp ground cardamom
    seeds
1.5ml/^{1}/$_4$ tsp ground paprika
1.5ml/^{1}/$_4$ tsp ground nutmeg
90ml/6 tbsp olive oil
salt and black pepper

1 Dry the chicken livers on kitchen paper, removing any unwanted pieces. Cut the large livers in half and leave the smaller ones whole.

2 Mix the flour with all the spices and the seasoning.

3 Coat a few of the livers with spiced flour, separating each piece. Heat the oil in a large frying pan and fry the livers in small batches. (This helps to keep the oil temperature high and prevents the flour from becoming soggy.)

4 Fry quickly, stirring frequently, until crispy. Keep warm and repeat with the remaining livers. Serve immediately with warm garlic bread and salad.

Mediterranean Tomato Soup

Children will love this soup –
especially if you use fancy pasta
shapes such as alphabet or animals.

Serves 4

675g/1¹/2 lb ripe plum tomatoes

1 medium onion, quartered

1 celery stick

1 garlic clove

15ml/1 tbsp olive oil

475ml/16fl oz/2 cups chicken stock

15ml/1 tbsp tomato purée

50g/2oz/¹/2 cup small pasta shapes

salt and black pepper

fresh coriander or parsley, to garnish

1 Put the tomatoes, onion, celery and garlic in a pan with the oil. Cover and cook over a low heat for 40–45 minutes, shaking the pan occasionally, until very soft.

2 Spoon the vegetables into a food processor or blender and process until smooth. Press through a sieve back into the pan.

3 Stir in the stock and tomato purée and bring to the boil. Add the pasta and simmer gently for about 8 minutes, or until the pasta is tender. Add salt and pepper, to taste, then sprinkle with coriander or parsley and serve hot.

Mushroom, Celery and Garlic Soup

Worcestershire sauce makes this
mushroom soup extra tasty.

Serves 4

350g/12oz/4¹/2 cups chopped mushrooms

4 celery sticks, chopped

3 garlic cloves

45ml/3 tbsp dry sherry or white wine

750ml/1¹/4 pints/3 cups chicken stock

30ml/2 tbsp Worcestershire sauce

5ml/1 tsp grated nutmeg

salt and black pepper

celery leaves, to garnish

1 Place the mushrooms, celery and garlic in a pan and stir in the sherry or wine. Cover and cook over a low heat for about 30–40 minutes, until tender.

2 Add half the stock and purée in a food processor or blender, until smooth. Return to the pan and add the remaining stock, the Worcestershire sauce and nutmeg.

3 Bring to the boil, season to taste and serve hot, garnished with celery leaves.

Chicken and Marsala Liver Pâté

This is a really quick and simple pâté to make, yet it has a delicious – and quite sophisticated – flavour. It contains Marsala, a soft and pungent fortified wine from Sicily. If it is unavailable, use brandy or a medium-dry sherry.

INGREDIENTS

Serves 4

350g/12oz chicken livers,
    defrosted if frozen
225g/8oz/1 cup butter, softened
2 garlic cloves, crushed
15ml/1 tbsp Marsala
5ml/1 tsp chopped fresh sage
salt and black pepper
8 sage leaves, to garnish
thin, crisp toast, to serve

1 Pick over the chicken livers, then rinse and dry with kitchen paper. Melt 25g/1oz/2 tbsp of the butter in a frying pan, and fry the chicken livers with the garlic over a medium heat for about 5 minutes, or until they are firm but still pink in the middle.

2 Transfer the livers to a blender or food processor, using a slotted spoon, and add the Marsala and chopped sage.

3 Melt 150g/5oz/10 tbsp of the remaining butter in the frying pan, stirring to loosen any sediment, then pour into the blender or processor and blend until smooth. Season well.

4 Spoon the pâté into four individual pots and smooth the surface. Melt the remaining butter in a separate pan and pour over the pâtés. Garnish with sage leaves and chill until set. Serve with triangles of toast.

Chicken Lettuce Parcels

Known as Sang Choy *in Hong Kong, this is a popular assemble-it-yourself treat. The filling – an imaginative blend of textures and flavours – is served with crisp lettuce leaves, which are used as wrappers.*

INGREDIENTS

Serves 6

2 chicken breast fillets, total weight about
    350g/12oz
4 dried Chinese mushrooms, soaked for
    30 minutes in warm water to cover
30ml/2 tbsp vegetable oil
2 garlic cloves, crushed
6 drained canned water chestnuts,
    thinly sliced
30ml/2 tbsp light soy sauce
5ml/1 tsp Sichuan peppercorns, dry-fried
    and crushed
4 spring onions, finely chopped
5ml/1 tsp sesame oil
vegetable oil, for deep-frying
50g/2oz cellophane noodles
salt and ground black pepper (optional)
1 crisp lettuce, divided into leaves, and
    60ml/4 tbsp hoisin sauce, to serve

1 Remove the skin from the chicken and set aside. Chop the chicken into thin strips. Drain the mushrooms, discard the stems, and slice the caps finely. Set aside.

2 Heat the oil in a wok or large frying pan. Add the garlic, then add the chicken, and stir-fry until the pieces are cooked through and no longer pink.

3 Add the mushrooms, water chestnuts, soy sauce and peppercorns. Toss for 2–3 minutes, then season, if needed. Stir in half the spring onions, then the sesame oil. Remove from the heat. Set aside.

4 Heat the oil to 190°C/375°F. Test by dropping a cube of bread into the oil: it should brown in 60 seconds. Cut the chicken skin into strips, deep-fry until crisp and drain. Add the noodles to the oil and deep-fry until crisp. Transfer to a plate lined with kitchen paper.

5 Crush the noodles and put in a serving dish. Top with the chicken skin, chicken mixture and the remaining spring onions. Arrange the lettuce leaves on a large platter.

6 Toss the chicken and noodles to mix. Each diner can take one or two lettuce leaves, spread the inside with hoisin sauce and add a spoonful of filling, turning in the sides of the leaves and rolling them into a parcel. The parcels are eaten held in the hand.

Chicken Cigars

These small crispy rolls can be served warm as canapés with a drink before a meal, or as a first course with a crisp, colourful salad.

Serves 4

275g/10oz packet of filo pastry
45ml/3 tbsp olive oil
fresh parsley, to garnish

For the filling
350g/12oz/3 cups minced raw chicken
salt and freshly ground black pepper
1 egg, beaten
2.5ml/$\frac{1}{2}$ tsp ground cinnamon
2.5ml/$\frac{1}{2}$ tsp ground ginger
30ml/2 tbsp raisins
15ml/1 tbsp olive oil
1 small onion, finely chopped

1 Mix all the filling ingredients, except the oil and onion, together in a bowl. Heat the oil in a large frying pan and cook the onion until tender. Leave to cool. Add the mixed filling ingredients.

2 Preheat the oven to 180°C/ 350°F/Gas 4. Once the filo pastry packet has been opened, keep the pastry covered at all times with a damp dish towel. Work fast, as the pastry dries out very quickly when exposed to the air. Unravel the pastry and cut into 25 x 10cm/ 10 x 4in strips.

3 Take a strip (cover the remainder), brush with a little oil and place a small spoonful of filling about 1cm/$\frac{1}{2}$in from the end.

4 To encase the filling, fold the sides inwards to a width of 5cm/2in and roll into a cigar shape. Place on a greased baking sheet and brush with oil. Repeat to use all the filling. Bake for about 20–25 minutes until golden brown and crisp. Garnish with fresh parsley and serve.

Chicken Roulades

These chicken rolls make a light lunch dish for two, or a starter for four. They can be sliced and served cold with a salad.

Makes 4

4 chicken thighs, boned and skinned
115g/4oz chopped fresh or frozen spinach
15g/^{1}/2oz/1 tbsp butter
25g/1oz/2 tbsp pine nuts
pinch of grated nutmeg
25g/1oz/7 tbsp fresh white breadcrumbs
4 rashers rindless streaky bacon
30ml/2 tbsp olive oil
150ml/^{1}/4 pint/^{2}/3 cup white wine
   or chicken stock
10ml/2 tsp cornflour
30ml/2 tbsp single cream
15ml/1 tbsp snipped fresh chives
salt and black pepper

1 Preheat the oven to 180°C/ 350°F/Gas 4. Place the chicken thighs between clear film and flatten with a rolling pin.

2 Put the spinach and butter into a saucepan, heat gently until the spinach has defrosted, if frozen, then increase the heat and cook rapidly, stirring occasionally until all the moisture has been driven off. Add the pine nuts, seasoning, nutmeg and fresh breadcrumbs.

3 Divide the filling between the chicken pieces and roll up neatly. Wrap a rasher of bacon around each piece and tie securely with fine string.

4 Heat the oil in a large frying pan and brown the rolls all over. Lift out using a slotted spoon to drain off the oil and place in a shallow ovenproof dish.

5 Pour over the wine or stock, cover, and bake for 15–20 minutes, or until tender. Transfer the chicken to a serving plate and remove the string. Strain the cooking liquid into a saucepan.

6 Blend the cornflour with a little cold water and add to the juices in the pan, along with the cream. Bring to the boil, stirring until thick. Adjust the seasoning and add the chives. Pour the sauce around the chicken and serve.

Chicken, Bacon and Walnut Terrine

To seal the terrine in the tin for longer storage, pour on melted lard.

Serves 8–10

2 boneless chicken breasts
1 large garlic clove, crushed
$^1/_2$ slice bread
1 egg
350g/12oz bacon chops (the fattier the better), minced or finely chopped
225g/8oz chicken or turkey livers, finely chopped
25g/1oz/$^1/_4$ cup chopped walnuts, toasted
30ml/2 tbsp sweet sherry or Madeira
2.5ml/$^1/_2$ tsp ground allspice
2.5ml/$^1/_2$ tsp cayenne pepper
pinch each ground nutmeg and cloves
8 long rashers streaky bacon, rind removed
salt and black pepper
chicory leaves and chives, to garnish

1 Cut the chicken breasts into thin strips and season lightly. Mash the garlic, bread and egg together. Work in the chopped bacon (using your hands is really the best way) and then the finely chopped livers. Stir in the chopped walnuts, sherry or Madeira, spices and seasoning to taste.

2 Preheat the oven to 200°C/400°F/Gas 6. Stretch each of the bacon rashers with a palette knife and use to line a 675g/1$^1/_2$lb loaf tin, then pack in half of the meat mixture.

3 Lay the chicken strips on the top and spread the rest of the mixture over. Cover the loaf tin with lightly-greased foil, seal well and press down very firmly.

4 Place the terrine in a roasting tin half-full of hot water and bake for 1–1$^1/_2$ hours, or until firm to the touch. Remove from the oven, place weights on the top and leave to cool completely. Drain off any excess fat or liquid while the terrine is warm.

5 When really cold, turn out the terrine, cut into thick slices and serve at once, garnished with a few chicory leaves and chives.

Mini Spring Rolls

Use a wok or a large frying pan for this recipe. For a spicier version, sprinkle with a little cayenne pepper.

INGREDIENTS

Makes 20

1 green chilli
120ml/4fl oz/$^1/_2$ cup vegetable oil
1 small onion, finely chopped
1 clove garlic, crushed
75g/3oz cooked chicken breast
1 small carrot, cut into fine matchsticks
1 spring onion, finely sliced
1 small red pepper, seeded and cut
    into fine matchsticks
25g/1oz beansprouts
15ml/1tbsp sesame oil
4 large sheets filo pastry
egg white, lightly beaten
long chives, to garnish (optional)
45ml/3 tbsp light soy sauce, to serve

1 Carefully remove the seeds from the chilli and chop finely, wearing rubber gloves to protect your hands, if necessary.

2 Heat the wok, then add 30ml/ 2 tbsp of the vegetable oil. When hot, add the onion, garlic and chilli. Stir-fry for 1 minute.

3 Slice the chicken thinly, then add to the wok and fry over a high heat, stirring and tossing constantly until browned.

4 Add the carrot, spring onion and red pepper and stir-fry for 2 minutes. Add the beansprouts, stir in the sesame oil, remove from the heat and leave to cool.

COOK'S TIP
〜

Always keep filo pastry sheets covered with a damp, clean cloth until needed, to prevent them drying out.

5 Cut each sheet of filo into 5 short strips. Place a small amount of filling at one end of each strip, then fold in the long sides and roll up the pastry. Seal and glaze the parcels with the egg white, then chill, uncovered, for 15 minutes before frying.

6 Wipe out the wok with kitchen paper, heat it, and add the remaining vegetable oil. When the oil is hot, fry the rolls in batches until crisp and golden brown. Drain on kitchen paper and serve dipped in light soy sauce.

Sesame Seed Chicken Bites

Stir-fry these crunchy bites in a wok, then serve them warm with a glass of chilled dry white wine.

Makes 20

175g/6oz raw chicken breast
2 cloves garlic, crushed
2.5cm/1in piece root ginger,
    peeled and grated
1 size 4 egg white
5ml/1 tsp cornflour
25g/1oz/¼ cup shelled pistachios,
    roughly chopped
60ml/4 tbsp sesame seeds
30ml/2 tbsp grapeseed oil
salt and black pepper

For the sauce
45ml/3 tbsp hoisin sauce
15ml/1 tbsp sweet chilli sauce

To garnish
fresh root ginger, finely shredded
pistachios, roughly chopped
fresh dill sprigs

1 Place the chicken, garlic, grated ginger, egg white and cornflour in a food processor or blender and process them to a smooth paste.

2 Stir in the pistachios and season with salt and pepper.

3 Roll into 20 balls and coat with sesame seeds. Heat the wok and add the oil. When the oil is hot, stir-fry the chicken bites in batches, turning regularly until golden. Drain on kitchen paper.

4 Make the sauce by mixing together the hoisin and chilli sauces in a bowl. Garnish the bites with shredded ginger, pistachios and dill. Serve hot, with a dish of sauce for dipping.

Spicy Chicken Canapés

*These tiny little cocktail sandwiches
have a spicy filling, and are finished
with different toppings. Use square
bread so that you can cut out more
rounds and have less wastage.*

INGREDIENTS

Makes 18

75g/3oz/³/4 cup finely chopped
    cooked chicken
2 spring onions, finely chopped
30ml/2 tbsp chopped red pepper
90ml/6 tbsp Curry Mayonnaise
6 slices white bread
15ml/1 tbsp paprika
15ml/1 tbsp chopped fresh parsley
30ml/2 tbsp chopped salted
    peanuts

2 Spread the mixture over three
of the bread slices and
sandwich with the remaining
bread, pressing well together.
Spread the remaining Curry
Mayonnaise over the top and cut
into 4cm/1¹/2in circles using a
plain cutter.

3 Dip into paprika, chopped
parsley or chopped nuts and
arrange attractively on a plate.

1 In a bowl mix the chopped
chicken with the chopped
spring onions, red pepper and half
the Curry Mayonnaise.

MIDWEEK
MEALS

Pancake Parcels

Making good use of the different types of minced poultry now available, these quick and easy pancakes are filled with a delicious chicken and apple mixture.

INGREDIENTS

Serves 4

For the filling

30ml/2 tbsp oil

450g/1lb/4 cups minced chicken

30ml/2 tbsp chopped fresh chives

2 green eating apples, cored and
   diced

25g/1oz/4 tbsp flour

175ml/6fl oz/³/4 cup chicken stock

salt and black pepper

For the pancakes

115g/4oz/1 cup plain flour

pinch of salt

1 egg, beaten

300ml/¹/2 pint/1¹/4 cups milk

oil for frying

For the sauce

60ml/4 tbsp cranberry sauce

50ml/2fl oz/¹/4 cup chicken stock

15ml/1 tbsp clear honey

15g/¹/2 oz/2 tbsp cornflour

1 To make the filling, heat the oil in a large pan and fry the chicken for 5 minutes. Add the chives and apples and then the flour. Stir in the stock and seasoning. Cook for 20 minutes.

2 To make the pancakes, sift the flour into a bowl together with a pinch of salt. Make a well in the centre and drop in the egg. Beat it in gradually with the milk to form a smooth batter. Heat the oil in a 15cm/6in omelette pan. Pour off the oil and add one-quarter of the pancake mixture. Tilt the pan to cover the base with the mixture and cook for 2–3 minutes. Turn the pancake over and cook for a further 2 minutes. Stack each pancake on top of one another and keep warm.

3 For the sauce, put the cranberry sauce, stock and honey into a pan. Heat gently until melted. Blend the cornflour with 20ml/4 tsp cold water, stir it in and bring to the boil. Cook, stirring until clear.

4 Lay the pancakes on a chopping board, spoon the filling into the centre and fold over around the filling. Put on a plate and spoon on the sauce. Serve with a fresh green vegetable.

Chicken Roule

A relatively simple dish to prepare, this recipe uses mince as a filling. It is rolled in chicken meat which is spread with a creamy garlic cheese that just melts in the mouth.

INGREDIENTS

Serves 4

4 boneless chicken breasts, about
    115g/4oz each
115g/4oz/1 cup minced beef
30ml/2 tbsp chopped fresh chives
225g/8oz Boursin or garlic
    cream cheese
30ml/2 tbsp clear honey
salt and black pepper

1 Preheat the oven to 190°C/
375°F/Gas 5. Place the chicken breasts, side by side, between two pieces of clear film. Beat with a meat mallet until 1cm/¹/₂in thick and joined together.

2 Place the minced beef in a large pan. Fry for 3 minutes, add the fresh chives and seasoning. Cool.

3 Place the chicken on a board and spread with the cream cheese.

4 Top with the mince mixture, spreading it over evenly.

5 Roll up the chicken tightly to form a sausage shape.

6 Brush with honey and place in a roasting tin. Cook for 1 hour in the preheated oven. Remove from the tin and slice thinly. Serve with freshly cooked vegetables.

Chicken with Apricot and Pecan Baskets

The potato baskets make a pretty addition to the chicken and could easily have different fillings when you feel the need for a change.

INGREDIENTS

Serves 8

8 chicken breast fillets, about 150g/5oz each
75g/3oz/6 tbsp butter
about 50g/2oz mushrooms, chopped
15g/^{1}/2oz/1 tbsp chopped pecan nuts
115g/4oz/^{2}/3 cup chopped, cooked ham
50g/2oz/1 cup wholemeal breadcrumbs
15ml/1 tbsp chopped parsley, plus some
 whole leaves to garnish
salt and black pepper
cocktail sticks to secure rolls

For the sauce

15ml/1 tbsp cornflour
120ml/4fl oz/^{1}/2 cup white wine
120ml/4fl oz/^{1}/2 cup chicken stock
50g/2oz/^{1}/4 cup apricot chutney

For the potato baskets

4 large baking potatoes, about 300g/11oz each
175g/6oz sausagemeat
225g/8oz can apricots in natural juice,
 drained and quartered
1.5ml/^{1}/4 tsp cinnamon
2.5ml/^{1}/2 tsp grated orange rind
30ml/2 tbsp maple syrup
25g/1oz/2 tbsp butter
35g/1^1/4oz/^{1}/4 cup chopped pecan nuts,
 plus some pecan halves to garnish

1 Preheat the oven to 200°C/400°F/Gas 6 and bake the potatoes for 1^1/2 hours, turning once, until soft. Meanwhile, put the chicken between two sheets of greaseproof paper and flatten with a meat mallet. Melt 25g/1oz/2 tbsp butter in a pan and sauté the mushrooms, pecans and ham. Stir in the breadcrumbs, parsley and seasoning. Divide the mixture between the chicken breasts, roll up and secure each one with a cocktail stick. Chill.

2 Mix the cornflour with a little of the wine to make a paste. Put the remaining wine and stock in a pan, and add the paste. Cook, stirring, until smooth. Add the remaining butter and the chutney and cook for 5 minutes, stirring constantly.

3 Turn down the oven to 180°C/350°F/Gas 4. Place the chicken breasts in a shallow ovenproof dish and pour over the sauce. Cover with foil and bake in the oven for 20–25 minutes until cooked.

4 When the potatoes are cooked, cut them in half and scoop out the inside. Mash the potato and place in a mixing bowl.

5 Fry the sausagemeat and drain off any fat. Add the remaining ingredients and cook for 1 minute. Mix together the sausagemeat and potato and put in the potato shells. Sprinkle the pecan halves over the top, put in the oven with the chicken and bake for 20–25 minutes.

6 Remove the chicken and drain the sauce into a separate dish. Slice the breasts, put on to plates and pour the sauce over the top. Serve with the potato baskets.

Chicken with Yellow Pepper Sauce

Escalopes of chicken filled with garlic cheese with yellow pepper sauce.

INGREDIENTS

Serves 4

30ml/2 tbsp olive oil

2 large yellow peppers, seeded and
   chopped

1 small onion, chopped

15ml/1 tbsp freshly squeezed orange juice

300ml/^{1}/$_2$ pint/1^1/$_4$ cups chicken stock

4 chicken breasts

75g/3oz Boursin or garlic cream cheese

12 fresh basil leaves

25g/1oz/2 tbsp butter

salt and black pepper

1 To make the yellow pepper sauce, heat half the oil in a pan and gently fry the peppers and onion until beginning to soften. Add the orange juice and stock and cook until very soft.

2 Meanwhile, lay the chicken fillets out flat and beat them out lightly.

3 Spread the chicken fillets with the Boursin or garlic cream cheese. Chop half the basil and sprinkle on top, then roll up the fillets, tucking in the ends like an envelope, and secure neatly with half a cocktail stick.

4 Heat the remaining oil and the butter in a frying pan and fry the fillets for 7–8 minutes, turning them frequently, until golden and cooked through.

5 While the fillets are cooking, press the pepper mixture through a sieve, or blend until smooth, then strain back into the pan. Season to taste and warm through, or serve cold, with the fillets, garnished with the remaining basil leaves.

COOK'S TIP

Turkey or veal escalopes could be
used in place of the chicken,
if you prefer.

Chilli Chicken Couscous

Couscous is a very easy alternative to rice and makes a good base for all kinds of ingredients.

INGREDIENTS

Serves 4

225g/8oz/2 cups couscous
1 litre/1³/4 pints/4 cups boiling water
5ml/1 tsp olive oil
400g/14oz chicken without
    skin and bone, diced
1 yellow pepper, seeded and sliced
2 large courgettes, sliced thickly
1 small green chilli, thinly sliced,
    or 5ml/1 tsp chilli sauce
1 large tomato, diced
425g/15oz can chick-peas, drained
salt and black pepper
coriander or parsley sprigs to garnish

1 Place the couscous in a large bowl and pour over boiling water. Cover and leave to stand for 30 minutes.

2 Heat the oil in a large, non-stick pan and stir-fry the chicken quickly to seal, then reduce the heat.

3 Stir in the pepper, courgettes and chilli or sauce and cook for about 10 minutes, until the vegetables are softened.

4 Stir in the tomato and chick-peas then add the couscous. Adjust the seasoning and stir over a moderate heat until hot. Serve garnished with sprigs of fresh coriander or parsley.

Chicken Bean Bake

Sliced aubergine layered with beans, chicken and topped with yogurt.

INGREDIENTS

Serves 4

1 medium aubergine, thinly sliced
15ml/1 tbsp olive oil, for brushing
450g/1lb boneless chicken breast, diced
1 medium onion, chopped
400g/14oz can chopped tomatoes
425g/15oz can red kidney beans, drained
15ml/1 tbsp paprika
15ml/1 tbsp chopped fresh thyme,
    or 5ml/1 tsp dried
5ml/1 tsp chilli sauce
350g/12oz/1¹/2 cups Greek-style yogurt
2.5ml/¹/2 tsp grated nutmeg
salt and black pepper

3 Remove the aubergine, add the chicken and onion to the pan, and cook until lightly browned. Stir in the tomatoes, beans, paprika, thyme, chilli sauce and seasoning. In a bowl, mix together the yogurt and grated nutmeg.

1 Preheat the oven to 190°C/375°F/Gas 5. Arrange the aubergine in a colander and sprinkle with salt.

2 Leave the aubergine for 30 minutes, then rinse and pat dry. Brush a non-stick pan with oil and fry the aubergine in batches, turning once, until golden.

4 Layer the meat and aubergine in an ovenproof dish, finishing with aubergine. Spread the yogurt evenly over the top and bake for 50–60 minutes, until golden.

Chicken Spirals

These little spirals look impressive, but they're very simple to make, and a good way to pep up plain chicken.

Serves 4

4 chicken breasts, about 90g/3^1/$_2$ oz
    each, thinly sliced

20ml/4 tsp tomato purée

15g/^{1}/$_2$ oz/^{1}/$_2$ cup large basil
    leaves

1 garlic clove, crushed

15ml/1 tbsp skimmed milk

30ml/2 tbsp wholemeal flour

salt and black pepper

passata or fresh tomato sauce and
    pasta, to serve

1 Place the chicken breasts on a board. If too thick, flatten them slightly by beating with a rolling pin or meat mallet.

2 Spread each chicken breast with tomato purée, then top with a few basil leaves, a little crushed garlic and seasoning.

3 Roll up firmly around the filling and secure with a cocktail stick. Brush with milk and sprinkle with flour to coat lightly.

4 Place the spirals on a foil-lined grill pan. Cook under a medium-hot grill for 15–20 minutes, turning them occasionally, until thoroughly cooked. Serve hot, sliced, with a spoonful or two of passata or fresh tomato sauce and accompanied with pasta sprinkled with fresh basil.

COOK'S TIP

When flattening the chicken breasts with a rolling pin, place them between two sheets of clear film.

Monday Savoury Omelette

Use up all the leftover odds and ends in this tasty omelette.

INGREDIENTS

Serves 4–6

30ml/2 tbsp olive oil

1 large onion, chopped

2 large garlic cloves, crushed

115g/4oz rindless bacon, chopped

50g/2oz cold cooked chicken, chopped

115g/4oz leftover cooked vegetables
   (preferably ones which are not too soft)

115g/4oz/1 cup leftover cooked
   rice or pasta

4 eggs

30ml/2 tbsp chopped, mixed fresh herbs,
   such as parsley, chives, marjoram or tarragon, or 10ml/2 tsp dried

5ml/1 tsp Worcestershire sauce,
   or more to taste

15ml/1 tbsp grated mature
   Cheddar cheese

salt and black pepper

1 Heat the oil in a large flame-proof frying pan and sauté the onion, garlic and bacon until all the fat has run out of the bacon.

2 Add the chopped meat, vegetables and rice. Beat the eggs, herbs and Worcestershire sauce together with seasoning. Pour over the rice or pasta and vegetables, stir lightly, then leave the mixture undisturbed to cook gently for about 5 minutes.

3 When just beginning to set, sprinkle with the cheese and place under a preheated grill until just firm and golden.

COOK'S TIP

This is surprisingly good cold, so is perfect for taking on picnics, or using for packed lunches.

Chicken Lasagne

Based on the Italian beef lasagne, this is an excellent dish for entertaining guests of all ages. Serve simply with a green salad.

Serves 8

30ml/2 tbsp olive oil

900g/2lb minced raw chicken

225g/8oz/1^1/2 cups rindless streaky bacon rashers, chopped

2 garlic cloves, crushed

450g/1lb leeks, sliced

225g/8oz/1^1/4 cups carrots, diced

30ml/2 tbsps tomato purée

475ml/16fl oz/2 cups chicken stock

12 sheets (no need to pre-cook) lasagne verde

For the cheese sauce

50g/2oz/4 tbsp butter

50g/2oz/^{1}/2 cup plain flour

600ml/1 pint/2^1/2 cups milk

115g/4oz/1 cup grated mature Cheddar cheese

1.5ml/^{1}/4 tsp dry English mustard

salt and black pepper

1 Heat the oil in a large flame-proof casserole dish and brown the minced chicken and bacon briskly, separating the pieces with a wooden spoon. Add the crushed garlic cloves, sliced leeks and diced carrots and cook for about 5 minutes until softened. Add the tomato purée, stock and seasoning. Bring to the boil, cover and simmer for 30 minutes.

2 To make the sauce, melt the butter in a saucepan, add the flour and gradually blend in the milk, stirring until smooth. Bring to the boil, stirring all the time until thickened and simmer for several minutes. Add half the grated cheese and the mustard and season to taste.

3 Preheat the oven to 190°C/375°F/Gas 5. Layer the chicken mixture, lasagne and half the cheese sauce in a 2.5 litre/5 pint ovenproof dish, starting and finishing with a layer of chicken.

4 Pour the remaining half of the cheese sauce over the top to cover, sprinkle over the remaining cheese and bake in the preheated oven for 1 hour, or until bubbling and lightly browned on top.

Crunchy Stuffed Chicken Breasts

These can be prepared ahead of time as long as the stuffing is quite cold before the chicken is stuffed. It is an ideal dish for entertaining.

Serves 4

4 chicken breasts, boned
25g/1oz/2 tbsp butter
1 garlic clove, crushed
15ml/1 tbsp Dijon mustard

For the stuffing
15g/^{1}/2 oz/1 tbsp butter
1 bunch spring onions, sliced
45ml/3 tbsp fresh breadcrumbs
25g/1oz/2 tbsp pine nuts
1 egg yolk
15ml/1 tbsp chopped fresh parsley
salt and black pepper
60ml/4 tbsp grated cheese

For the topping
2 bacon rashers, finely chopped
50g/2oz/1 cup fresh breadcrumbs
15ml/1 tbsp grated Parmesan cheese
15ml/1 tbsp chopped fresh parsley

1 Preheat the oven to 200°C/ 400°F/Gas 6. To make the stuffing, heat 15g/^{1}/2 oz/1 tbsp of the butter in a frying pan and cook the spring onions until soft. Remove from the heat and allow to cool for a few minutes.

2 Add the remaining ingredients and mix thoroughly.

3 To make the topping, fry the chopped bacon until crispy, drain and add to the breadcrumbs, Parmesan cheese and fresh parsley.

4 Carefully cut a deep pocket in each of the chicken breasts, using a sharp knife.

5 Divide the stuffing into four and use to fill the pockets. Put in a buttered ovenproof dish.

6 Melt the remaining butter, mix it with the crushed garlic and mustard, and brush liberally over the chicken. Press on the topping and bake uncovered for about 30–40 minutes, or until tender.

Chicken with Honey and Grapefruit

Chicken breast portions cook very quickly and are ideal for suppers "on-the-run" – but don't be tempted to overcook them. You could substitute boneless turkey steaks or duck breast fillets for the chicken, if you prefer.

INGREDIENTS

Serves 4

4 chicken breast portions, skinned

45–60ml/3–4 tbsp clear honey

1 pink grapefruit, skinned and
    cut into 12 segments

salt and black pepper

noodles and salad leaves, to serve

1 Make three quite deep, diagonal slits in the chicken flesh using a large sharp knife.

2 Brush the chicken all over with the honey and sprinkle well with seasoning.

3 Put the chicken in a flameproof dish, uncut side uppermost, and place under a medium grill for 2–3 minutes.

4 Turn the chicken over and place the grapefruit segments in the slits. Brush with more honey and cook for a further 5 minutes, or until tender. If necessary, reduce the heat so that the honey glaze does not burn. Serve at once with noodles and salad leaves.

Crispy Chicken with Garlic Rice

Chicken wings cooked until they are really tender have a surprising amount of meat on them, and make a very economical supper for a crowd of youngsters – provide lots of kitchen paper, napkins and finger bowls for the sticky fingers.

INGREDIENTS

Serves 4

1 large onion, chopped

2 garlic cloves, crushed

30ml/2 tbsp sunflower oil

175g/6oz/1¼ cups basmati rice

350ml/12fl oz/1½ cups hot chicken stock

10ml/2 tsp finely grated lemon rind

30ml/2 tbsp chopped mixed herbs

8 or 12 chicken wings

50g/2oz/½ cup plain flour

salt and black pepper

fresh tomato sauce and
    vegetables, to serve

1 Preheat the oven to 200°C/ 400°F/Gas 6. Fry the onion and garlic in the oil in a large flameproof casserole, until golden. Stir in the rice and toss until all the grains are well coated in oil.

2 Stir in the stock, lemon rind and herbs and bring to the boil. Cover and cook in the middle of the oven for 40–50 minutes. Stir once or twice during cooking.

3 Meanwhile, wipe dry the chicken wings. Season the flour and use to coat the chicken portions thoroughly.

4 Put the chicken wings in a small roasting tin and cook in the top of the oven for 30–40 minutes, turning once, until crispy.

5 Serve the rice and chicken wings with a fresh tomato sauce and a selection of vegetables.

Thai Chicken and Vegetable Stir-fry

Make this speedy dish a little hotter by adding more fresh root ginger.

INGREDIENTS

Serves 4

1 piece lemon grass (or the rind of
 $^1/_2$ lemon), cut in thin slices
1cm/$^1/_2$ in piece of fresh
 root ginger
1 large garlic clove
30ml/2 tbsp sunflower oil
275g/10oz lean chicken, thinly sliced
$^1/_2$ red pepper, seeded and sliced
$^1/_2$ green pepper, seeded and sliced
4 spring onions, chopped
2 medium carrots, cut into matchsticks
115g/4oz fine green beans
30ml/2 tbsp oyster sauce
pinch sugar
salt and black pepper
25g/1oz/$^1/_4$ cup salted peanuts,
 lightly crushed, and coriander
 leaves, to garnish
cooked rice, to serve

1 Thinly slice the lemon grass or lemon rind. Peel and chop the ginger and garlic. Heat the oil in a frying pan over a high heat. Add the lemon grass or lemon rind, ginger and garlic, and stir-fry for 30 seconds until brown.

2 Add the chicken and stir-fry for 2 minutes. Then add the vegetables and stir-fry for 4–5 minutes, until the chicken is cooked and the vegetables are almost cooked.

3 Finally stir in the oyster sauce, sugar and seasoning to taste and stir-fry for another minute to mix and blend well. Serve at once, sprinkled with the peanuts and coriander leaves and accompanied with cooked rice.

Chicken with Herbs and Lentils

*Chicken baked on lentils and served
topped with garlic butter.*

Serves 4

115g/4oz piece of thick bacon or belly
    pork, rind removed, chopped

1 large onion, sliced

475ml/16fl oz/2 cups well-flavoured
    chicken stock

bay leaf

2 sprigs each parsley, marjoram and
    thyme

225g/8oz/1 cup green or brown lentils

4 chicken portions

salt and black pepper

25–50g/1–2oz/2–4 tbsp garlic butter

COOK'S TIP

For economy buy a smallish
chicken and cut it in quarters, to
give generous portions.

1 Fry the bacon gently in a large,
heavy-based flameproof
casserole until all the fat runs out
and the bacon begins to brown.
Add the onion and fry for about
another 2 minutes.

2 Stir in the chicken stock, bay
leaf, herb stalks and some of
the leafy parts (keep some herb
sprigs for garnish), lentils and seasoning. Preheat the oven to
190°C/375°F/ Gas 5.

3 Fry the chicken portions in a
frying pan to brown the skin
before placing on top of the lentils.
Sprinkle with seasoning and some
of the herbs.

4 Cover the casserole and cook
in the oven for about 40
minutes. Serve with a knob of
garlic butter on each portion and a
few of the remaining herb sprigs.

Minty Yogurt Chicken

Chicken marinated with yogurt,
mint, lemon and honey and grilled.

Serves 4

8 chicken thigh portions, skinned

15ml/1 tbsp clear honey

30ml/2 tbsp lime or lemon juice

30ml/2 tbsp natural yogurt

60ml/4 tbsp chopped fresh mint

salt and black pepper

new potatoes and a tomato salad,
    to serve

1 Slash the chicken flesh at regular intervals with a sharp knife. Place in a bowl.

2 Mix together the honey, lime or lemon juice, yogurt, seasoning and half the mint.

3 Spoon the marinade over the chicken and leave to marinate for 30 minutes. Line the grill pan with foil and cook the chicken under a moderately hot grill until thoroughly cooked and golden brown, turning the chicken occasionally during cooking.

4 Sprinkle with the remaining mint and serve with the potatoes and tomato salad.

Oat-crusted Chicken with Sage

Oats make a good coating for savoury foods, and offer a good way to add extra fibre.

INGREDIENTS

Serves 4

45ml/3 tbsp skimmed milk
10ml/2 tsp English mustard
40g/1^{1}/2oz/^{1}/2 cup rolled oats
45ml/3 tbsp chopped sage leaves
8 chicken thighs or drumsticks, skinned
115g/4oz/^{1}/2 cup low-fat fromage frais
5ml/1 tsp wholegrain mustard
salt and black pepper
fresh sage leaves, to garnish

COOK'S TIP

If fresh sage is not available, choose another fresh herb, such as thyme or parsley, rather than a dried alternative.

1 Preheat the oven to 200°C/ 400°F/Gas 6. Mix together the milk and English mustard.

2 Mix the oats with 30ml/2 tbsp of the sage and the seasoning on a plate. Brush the chicken with the milk and press into the oats.

3 Place the chicken on a baking sheet and bake for about 40 minutes, or until the juices run clear, not pink, when pierced through the thickest part.

4 Meanwhile, mix together the low-fat fromage frais, whole-grain mustard, remaining sage and seasoning, then serve with the chicken. Garnish the chicken with fresh sage and serve hot or cold.

Tagine of Chicken

Based on a traditional Moroccan dish. The chicken and couscous can be cooked the day before and reheated for serving.

Serves 8

8 chicken legs (thighs and drumsticks)
30ml/2 tbsp olive oil
1 medium onion, finely chopped
2 garlic cloves, crushed
5ml/1 tsp ground turmeric
2.5ml/^{1}/$_2$ tsp ground ginger
2.5ml/^{1}/$_2$ tsp ground cinnamon
475ml/16fl oz/2 cups chicken stock
150g/5oz/1^1/$_4$ cups stoned green olives
1 lemon, sliced
salt and black pepper
fresh coriander sprigs, to garnish

For the vegetable couscous
600ml/1 pint/2^1/$_2$ cups chicken stock
450g/1lb couscous
4 courgettes, thickly sliced
2 carrots, thickly sliced
2 small turnips, peeled and cubed
45ml/3 tbsp olive oil
450g/1lb can chick-peas, drained
15ml/1 tbsp chopped fresh coriander

1 Preheat the oven to 180°C/ 350°F/Gas 4. Cut the chicken legs into two through the joint.

2 Heat the oil in a large flame-proof casserole and, working in batches, brown the chicken on both sides. Drain and remove to a dish and keep warm.

3 Add the onion and crushed garlic to the flameproof casserole and cook gently until tender. Add the spices and cook for 1 minute. Pour over the stock, bring to the boil, and return the chicken. Cover and bake for 45 minutes until tender. Transfer the chicken to a dish, cover and keep warm.

4 Remove any fat from the cooking liquid and boil to reduce by one-third. Meanwhile, blanch the olives and lemon slices in a pan of boiling water for 2 minutes until the lemon skin is tender. Drain and add to the cooking liquid, adjusting the seasoning to taste.

5 To cook the couscous, bring the stock to the boil in a large pan and sprinkle in the couscous slowly, stirring all the time. Remove from the heat, cover and leave to stand for 5 minutes.

6 Meanwhile, cook the prepared vegetables, drain and put them into a large bowl. Add the couscous and oil and season. Stir the grains to fluff them up, add the chick-peas and finally the chopped coriander. Spoon on to a large serving plate, cover with the chicken, and spoon over the liquid. Garnish with the fresh coriander.

Chicken with Asparagus

Canned asparagus may be used instead of fresh, but will not require any cooking – simply add at the very end to warm through.

INGREDIENTS

Serves 4

4 large chicken breasts, boned and
   skinned
15ml/1 tbsp ground coriander
30ml/2 tbsp olive oil
20 slender asparagus spears, cut
   into 7.5–10cm/3–4 in lengths
300ml/^{1}/$_2$ pint/1^1/$_4$ cups chicken stock
15ml/1 tbsp cornflour
15ml/1 tbsp lemon juice
salt and black pepper
15ml/1 tbsp chopped fresh parsley

1 Divide the chicken breasts into two natural fillets. Place each between two sheets of clear film and flatten to a thickness of 5mm/^{1}/$_4$ in with a rolling pin. Cut into 2.5cm/1in strips diagonally. Sprinkle over the coriander and toss to coat each piece.

2 Heat the oil in a large frying pan and fry the chicken very quickly in small batches for 3–4 minutes until lightly coloured. Season each batch with a little salt and freshly ground black pepper. Remove and keep warm while frying the rest of the chicken.

3 Add the asparagus and chicken stock to the pan and bring to the boil. Cook for a further 4–5 minutes, or until tender.

4 Mix the cornflour to a paste with a little cold water and stir into the sauce to thicken. Return the chicken to the pan and add the lemon juice. Reheat and then serve immediately, garnished with fresh parsley.

Chicken, Carrot and Leek Parcels

These intriguing parcels may sound a bit fiddly for everyday, but they take very little time and you can freeze them – ready to cook gently from frozen.

INGREDIENTS

Serves 4

4 chicken fillets or boneless breasts

2 small leeks, sliced

2 carrots, grated

4 stoned black olives, chopped

1 garlic clove, crushed

15–30ml/1–2 tbsp olive oil

8 anchovy fillets

salt and black pepper

black olives and herb sprigs, to garnish

1 Preheat the oven to 200°C/ 400°F/Gas 6. Season the chicken well with salt and pepper.

2 Divide the leeks equally among four sheets of greased grease-proof paper, about 23cm/9in square. Place a piece of chicken on top of each one.

3 Mix the carrots, olives, garlic and oil together. Season lightly and place on top of the chicken portions. Top each with two of the anchovy fillets, then carefully wrap up each parcel, making sure the paper folds are underneath and the carrot mixture on top.

4 Bake for 20 minutes and serve hot, in the paper, garnished with black olives and herb sprigs.

Chicken in a Tomato Coat

Chicken roasted with a coating of tomato sauce and fresh tomatoes.

INGREDIENTS

Serves 4–6

1.5–1.75kg/3–4^{1}/2lb free-range chicken

1 small onion

knob of butter

75ml/5 tbsp ready-made tomato sauce

30ml/2 tbsp chopped, mixed fresh herbs, such as parsley, tarragon, sage, basil and marjoram, or 10ml/2 tsp dried

small glass of dry white wine

2–3 small tomatoes, sliced

olive oil

little cornflour (optional)

salt and black pepper

1 Preheat the oven to 190°C/ 375°F/Gas 5. Place the chicken in a roasting tin. Place the onion, the knob of butter and some seasoning inside the chicken.

2 Spread most of the tomato sauce over the chicken and sprinkle with half the herbs and some seasoning. Pour the wine into the roasting tin.

3 Cover with foil, then roast for 1^{1}/2 hours, basting occasion-ally. Remove the foil, spread with the remaining sauce and the sliced tomatoes and drizzle with oil. Continue cooking for a further 20–30 minutes, or until the chicken is cooked through.

4 Sprinkle the remaining herbs over the chicken, then carve into portions. Thicken the sauce with a little cornflour if you wish.

Chicken Stroganov

*Based on the classic Russian dish,
usually made with fillet of beef.
Serve with rice mixed with chopped
celery and spring onions.*

INGREDIENTS

Serves 4

4 large chicken breasts, boned and
   skinned
45ml/3 tbsp olive oil
1 large onion, thinly sliced
225g/8oz/3 cups mushrooms, sliced
300ml/^{1}/$_2$ pint/1^1/$_4$ cups soured cream
salt and black pepper
15ml/1 tbsp chopped fresh parsley,
   to garnish

1 Divide the chicken breasts into
two natural fillets, place
between two sheets of clear film
and flatten each to a thickness of
1cm/^{1}/$_2$in with a rolling pin.

2 Cut into 2.5cm/1in strips
diagonally across the fillets.

3 Heat 30ml/2 tbsp of the oil in a
frying pan and cook the onion
slowly until soft but not coloured.

4 Add the mushrooms and cook
until golden brown. Remove
and keep warm.

5 Increase the heat, add the
remaining oil and fry the
chicken very quickly, in small
batches, for 3–4 minutes until
lightly coloured. Remove to a dish
and keep warm.

6 Return all the chicken, onions
and mushrooms to the pan and
season with salt and black pepper.
Stir in the soured cream and bring
to the boil. Sprinkle with fresh
parsley and serve immediately.

Chicken Pancakes

A good way of using up leftover cooked chicken and bought pancakes.

Serves 4

225g/8oz cooked, boned chicken
25g/1oz/2 tbsp butter
1 small onion, finely chopped
50g/2oz mushrooms, finely
 chopped
30ml/2 tbsp plain flour
150ml/^{1}/4 pint/^{2}/3 cup chicken
 stock or milk
15ml/1 tbsp chopped fresh parsley
8 small or 4 large cooked pancakes
oil, for brushing
30ml/2 tbsp grated cheese
salt and black pepper

1 Remove the skin from the chicken and cut into cubes.

2 Heat the butter in a saucepan and cook the onion gently until tender. Add the mushrooms. Cook, covered, for a further 3–4 minutes.

3 Add the flour and then the stock or milk, stirring continually. Boil to thicken and simmer for 2 minutes. Season with salt and black pepper.

4 Add the chicken cubes and chopped fresh parsley.

5 Divide the filling equally between the pancakes, roll them up and arrange in a greased ovenproof dish. Preheat the grill.

6 Brush the pancakes with a little oil and sprinkle with cheese. Grill until browned. Serve hot.

Lemon Chicken Stir-fry

It is essential to prepare all the ingredients before you begin so they are ready to cook. This dish is cooked in minutes.

INGREDIENTS

Serves 4

4 chicken breasts, boned and skinned
15ml/1 tbsp light soy sauce
75ml/5 tbsp cornflour
1 bunch spring onions
1 lemon
1 garlic clove, crushed
15ml/1 tbsp caster sugar
30ml/2 tbsp sherry
150ml/^{1}/4 pint/^{2}/3 cup chicken stock
60ml/4 tbsp olive oil
salt and black pepper

1 Divide the chicken breasts into two natural fillets. Place each between two sheets of clear film and flatten to a thickness of 5mm/^{1}/4 in with a rolling pin.

2 Cut into 2.5cm/1in strips across the grain of the fillets. Put in a bowl with the soy sauce and toss to coat. Sprinkle on 60ml/ 4 tbsp of the cornflour and toss.

3 Trim off the roots and cut the spring onions diagonally into 1cm/^{1}/2in pieces. With a swivel peeler, remove the lemon rind in thin strips and cut into fine shreds, or grate finely. Reserve the lemon juice. Have ready the garlic, sugar, sherry, stock, lemon juice and remaining cornflour blended to a paste with water.

4 Heat the oil in a wok or large frying pan and cook the chicken very quickly in small batches for 3–4 minutes until lightly coloured. Remove to a dish and keep warm.

5 Add the spring onions and garlic to the pan and cook for 2 minutes.

6 Add the remaining ingredients, with chicken, and bring to the boil, stirring until thickened. Add more sherry or stock if necessary and stir until the chicken is evenly covered with sauce. Reheat for about 2 minutes.

Crispy Spring Chickens

These small birds can be roasted in the oven fairly quickly and are delicious either hot or cold.

Serves 4

2 x 900g/2lb chickens
salt and black pepper

For the honey glaze
30ml/2 tbsp clear honey
30ml/2 tbsp sherry
15ml/1 tbsp vinegar

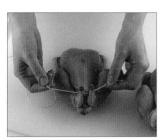

1 Preheat the oven to 180°C/ 350°F/Gas 4. Tie the birds into a neat shape and place on a wire rack over the sink. Pour over boiling water to plump the flesh and pat dry with kitchen paper.

2 Mix the honey, sherry and vinegar together and brush over the birds. Season well.

3 Put the rack into a roasting tin and roast the birds for 45–55 minutes. Baste well during cooking with the honey glaze until crisp and golden brown.

Chicken Cordon Bleu

A rich dish, popular with cheese lovers. Serve simply with green beans and tiny baked potatoes, cut and filled with cream cheese.

INGREDIENTS

Serves 4

4 chicken breasts, boned and
    skinned
4 slices cooked lean ham
60ml/4 tbsp grated Gruyère or
    Emmental cheese
30ml/2 tbsp olive oil
115g/4oz button mushrooms, sliced
60ml/4 tbsp white wine
salt and black pepper
watercress, to garnish

1 Place the chicken between two pieces of clear film and flatten to a thickness of 5mm/¼in with a rolling pin. Place the chicken breasts, outer side down, on the board and lay a slice of ham on each. Divide the cheese between the chicken and season with a little salt and freshly ground pepper.

2 Fold the chicken breasts in half and secure with wooden cocktail sticks, making a large "stitch" to hold the pieces together.

3 Heat the oil in a large frying pan and brown the chicken parcels on all sides. Remove to a dish and keep warm.

4 Add the mushrooms to the pan and cook for several minutes to brown lightly. Replace the chicken and pour over the wine, cover, and cook gently for 15–20 minutes until tender. Remove the cocktail sticks and arrange on a serving dish with a bunch of watercress.

Chicken in Herb Crusts

The chicken breasts can be brushed with melted butter instead of mustard before being coated in the breadcrumb mixture. Serve with new potatoes and salad.

INGREDIENTS

Serves 4

4 chicken breasts, boned and skinned
15ml/1 tbsp Dijon mustard
50g/2oz/1 cup fresh breadcrumbs
30ml/2 tbsp chopped fresh parsley
15ml/1 tbsp mixed dried herbs
25g/1oz/2 tbsp butter, melted
salt and black pepper

2 Mix the breadcrumbs and herbs together thoroughly.

3 Press on to the chicken to coat. Spoon over the melted butter. Bake uncovered for 20 minutes or until tender and crisp.

1 Preheat the oven to 180°C/ 350°F/Gas 4. Lay the chicken breasts in a greased ovenproof dish and spread with the mustard. Season with salt and freshly ground black pepper.

Tandoori Chicken Kebabs

This dish originates from the plains of the Punjab at the foot of the Himalayas. There food is tradition-ally cooked in clay ovens known as tandoors – hence the name.

Serves 4

4 chicken breasts, about 175g/6oz each,
   boned and skinned
15ml/1 tbsp lemon juice
45ml/3 tbsp tandoori paste
45ml/3 tbsp natural yogurt
1 garlic clove, crushed
30ml/2 tbsp chopped fresh coriander
1 small onion, cut into wedges and
   separated into layers
a little oil, for brushing
salt and black pepper
fresh coriander sprigs, to garnish
pilau rice and naan bread, to serve

1 Chop the chicken breasts into 2.5cm/1in cubes, place in a bowl and add the lemon juice, tandoori paste, yogurt, garlic, coriander and seasoning. Cover and leave to marinate in the fridge for at least 2–3 hours.

2 Preheat the grill. Thread alternate pieces of chicken and onion on to four skewers.

3 Brush the onions with a little oil, lay the kebabs on a grill rack and cook under a high heat for about 10–12 minutes, turning once. Garnish the kebabs with fresh coriander and serve at once with pilau rice and naan bread.

Chinese Chicken with Cashew Nuts

A stir-fry of chicken with egg noodles, spring onions and cashews.

Serves 4

4 chicken breasts about 175g/6oz each,
   boned, skinned and sliced into strips
3 garlic cloves, crushed
60ml/4 tbsp soy sauce
30ml/2 tbsp cornflour
225g/8oz/1 cup dried egg noodles
45ml/3 tbsp groundnut or sunflower oil
15ml/1 tbsp sesame oil
115g/4oz/1 cup roasted cashew nuts
6 spring onions, cut into 5cm/2in pieces
   and halved lengthways
spring onion curls and a little chopped
   red chilli, to garnish

4 Add the cashew nuts and spring onions to the pan or wok and stir-fry for 2–3 minutes.

1 Mix the chicken, garlic, soy sauce and cornflour in a bowl. Cover and chill for 30 minutes.

2 Bring a pan of water to the boil and add the noodles. Turn off the heat and leave to stand for 5 minutes. Drain well and reserve.

3 Heat the oils in a large frying pan and add the chicken and marinade. Stir-fry for about 3–4 minutes, or until golden brown.

5 Add the drained noodles and stir-fry for a further 2 minutes. Serve immediately, garnished with the spring onion curls and chopped red chilli.

Spatchcock of Poussins

*Allow one poussin per person. Serve
with boiled new potatoes and salad.*

INGREDIENTS

Serves 4

4 poussins

50g/2oz/4 tbsp butter, melted

15ml/1 tbsp lemon juice

15ml/1 tbsp chopped mixed fresh herbs,
 e.g. rosemary and parsley, plus
 extra to garnish

salt and black pepper

lemon slices, to garnish

1 Remove any trussing strings
and, using a pair of kitchen
scissors, cut down on either side of
the backbone and remove it. Lay
the poussins flat and flatten with
the help of a rolling pin or mallet.

2 Thread the legs and wings on
to skewers to keep the poussins
flat while they are cooking.

3 Brush both sides with melted
butter and season with salt and
pepper to taste. Sprinkle with
lemon juice and herbs.

4 Preheat the grill to medium
heat and cook skin-side first
for 6 minutes until golden brown.
Turn over, brush with butter and
grill for a further 6–8 minutes or
until cooked. Garnish with more
chopped herbs and lemon slices.

Poussins Véronique

Double poussins are eight to ten weeks old and are large enough to serve two people.

Serves 4

2 double poussins

2 fresh tarragon or thyme sprigs

25g/1oz/2 tbsp butter

60ml/4 tbsp white wine

grated rind and juice of $^1/_2$ lemon

15ml/1 tbsp olive oil

15ml/1 tbsp plain flour

150ml/$^1/_4$ pint/$^2/_3$ cup chicken stock

115g/4oz seedless green grapes,
    cut in half if large

salt and black pepper

chopped fresh parsley, to garnish

1 Preheat the oven to 180°C/ 350°F/Gas 4. Put the herbs inside the cavity of each poussin and tie into a neat shape.

2 Heat the butter in a casserole, brown the poussins lightly all over and pour on the wine. Season, cover, and cook in the oven for 20–30 minutes or until tender.

3 Remove the poussins from the casserole and cut in half with a pair of kitchen scissors, removing the backbones and small rib cage bones. Arrange in a shallow oven-proof dish (that will slide under the grill). Sprinkle with lemon juice and brush with oil. Grill until lightly browned. Keep warm.

4 Mix the flour into the butter and wine in the casserole, and blend in the stock. Bring to the boil, season to taste and add the lemon rind and grapes, then simmer for 2–3 minutes. Spoon the sauce over the poussins, garnish with fresh parsley and serve immediately.

Chicken with Orange and Mustard Sauce

The beauty of this recipe is its simplicity; the chicken continues to cook in its own juices while you prepare the sauce.

INGREDIENTS

Serves 4

2 large oranges

4 chicken breasts, boned and skinned

5ml/1 tsp sunflower oil

salt and black pepper

new potatoes and sliced courgettes
   tossed in parsley, to serve

Orange and mustard sauce

10ml/2 tsp cornflour

150ml/^{1}/4 pint/^{2}/3 cup natural yogurt

5ml/1 tsp Dijon mustard

1 Peel the oranges using a sharp knife, removing all the white pith. Remove the segments by cutting between the membranes, holding the fruit over a small bowl to catch any juice. Set aside with the juice until required.

2 Season the chicken with salt and freshly ground black pepper. Heat the oil in a non-stick frying pan and cook the chicken breasts for 5 minutes on each side. Take out of the frying pan and wrap in foil; the meat will continue to cook for a while.

3 To make the sauce, blend together the cornflour with the juice from the orange. Add the yogurt and mustard. Put into the frying pan and slowly bring to the boil. Simmer for 1 minute.

4 Add the orange segments to the sauce and heat gently. Unwrap the chicken and add any excess juices to the sauce. Slice on the diagonal and serve with the sauce, new potatoes and sliced courgettes tossed in parsley.

Chicken and Chorizo

*The perfect way to use up leftover
cold meat – this spicy dish is a fast,
fortifying meal for a hungry family.*

INGREDIENTS

Serves 4

45ml/3 tbsp vegetable oil

1 medium onion, chopped

1 celery stick, chopped

^{1}/2 red pepper, chopped

400g/14oz/2 cups long-grain rice

1 litre/1^3/4 pints/4 cups chicken stock

15ml/1 tbsp tomato purée

3–4 shakes of Tabasco sauce

225g/8oz cold roast chicken or pork,
    thickly sliced

115g/4oz cooked sausage, such as chorizo
    or kabanos, sliced

75g/3oz frozen peas

3 Stir in the cold meat, sausage
and peas and simmer for a
further 5 minutes. Switch off the
heat, cover and leave to stand for 5
minutes more before serving.

VARIATION

You could also add cooked ham,
smoked cod or haddock and fresh
shellfish to this dish.

1 Heat the oil in a heavy-based
saucepan and add the onion,
celery and pepper. Cook to soften
without colouring.

2 Add the rice, chicken stock,
tomato purée and Tabasco
sauce. Simmer uncovered for
about 10 minutes.

Chicken Cutlets with Olives

This quick and tasty dish makes a good light main course.

INGREDIENTS

Serves 4

90ml/6 tbsp olive oil

1 clove garlic, peeled and lightly
    crushed

1 dried chilli, lightly crushed

500g/1¼ lb boneless chicken breast,
    cut into 5mm/¼ in slices

100ml/4fl oz/½ cup dry white wine

4 tomatoes, peeled and seeded,
    cut into thin strips

about 24 black olives

6–8 leaves fresh basil, torn into pieces

salt and black pepper

1 Heat 60ml/4 tbsp of the olive oil in a large frying pan. Add the garlic and crushed dried chilli, and cook over low heat until the garlic is golden.

2 Raise the heat to moderate and add the remaining oil. Place the chicken slices in the pan, and brown them lightly on both sides for about 2 minutes. Season with salt and pepper. Remove the chicken to a heated dish.

3 Discard the garlic and chilli. Add the wine, tomato strips and olives. Cook over moderate heat for 3–4 minutes, scraping up any meat residue from the bottom of the pan.

4 Return the chicken to the pan. Sprinkle with the torn basil. Heat through for 30 seconds, and serve at once.

Mediterranean Chicken Skewers

These skewers are easy to assemble, and can be cooked on a grill or charcoal barbecue.

INGREDIENTS

Serves 4

90ml/6 tbsp olive oil

45ml/3 tbsp fresh lemon juice

1 clove garlic, finely chopped

30ml/2 tbsp chopped fresh basil

2 medium courgettes

1 long thin aubergine

300g/11oz boneless chicken, cut into
    5cm/2in cubes

12–16 pickled onions

1 pepper, red or yellow, cut into
    5cm/2in squares

salt and black pepper

1 In a small bowl mix the oil with the lemon juice, garlic and basil. Season with salt and pepper.

2 Slice the courgettes and aubergine lengthways into strips 5mm/¼in thick. Cut them crossways about two-thirds of the way along their length. Discard the shorter length. Wrap half the chicken pieces with the courgette slices, and the other half with the aubergine slices.

3 Prepare the skewers by alternating the chicken, onions and pepper pieces. Lay the prepared skewers on a platter, and sprinkle with the flavoured oil. Leave to marinate for at least 30 minutes. Preheat the grill, or prepare a barbecue.

4 Grill or barbecue for about 10 minutes, or until the vegetables are tender, turning the skewers occasionally. Serve hot.

Poussins with Dirty Rice

This rice is called dirty not because of the bits in it (though the roux and chicken livers do "muss" it up a bit) but because jazz is called "dirty music", and the rice in this recipe is certainly jazzed up.

INGREDIENTS

Serves 4

For the rice

60ml/4 tbsp cooking oil

25g/1oz/¹/4 cup plain flour

50g/2oz/4 tbsp butter

1 large onion, chopped

2 celery sticks, chopped

1 green pepper, seeded and diced

2 garlic cloves, crushed

200g/7oz minced pork

225g/8oz chicken livers, trimmed and sliced

Tabasco sauce

300ml/¹/2 pint/1¹/4 cups chicken stock

4 spring onions, shredded

45ml/3 tbsp chopped fresh parsley

225g/8oz/generous 1 cup American long-grain rice, cooked

salt and black pepper

For the birds

4 poussins

2 bay leaves, halved

25g/1oz/2 tbsp butter

1 lemon

COOK'S TIP
❧

You can substitute quails for the poussins, in which case offer two per person and stuff each little bird with 10ml/2 tsp of the dirty rice before roasting for about 20 minutes.

---

1 In a small heavy-based pan, make a roux by blending together 2 tbsp of the oil and the flour. When it is a chestnut brown colour, remove the pan from the heat and place it immediately on a cold surface.

2 Heat the remaining 2 tbsp oil with the butter in a frying pan and stir-fry the onion, celery and green pepper for about 5 minutes.

3 Add the garlic and pork and stir-fry for about 5 minutes, breaking up the pork and stirring well to cook it all over.

4 Add the chicken livers and fry for 2–3 minutes until they have changed colour all over. Season with salt and black pepper and a dash of Tabasco sauce.

5 Stir the roux into the stir-fried mixture, then gradually add the stock. When it begins to bubble, cover and cook for 30 minutes, stirring occasionally. Uncover and cook for a further 15 minutes, stirring frequently.

6 Preheat the oven to 200°C/400°F/Gas 6. Mix the shredded spring onions and chopped parsley into the meat mixture and stir it all into the cooked rice.

7 Put ¹/2 bay leaf and 1 tbsp rice into each poussin. Rub the outside with the butter and season with salt and pepper.

8 Put the birds on a rack in a roasting tin, squeeze the juice from the lemon over them and roast in the oven for 35–40 minutes, basting twice during cooking with the pan juices.

9 Put the remaining rice into a shallow ovenproof dish, cover it and place on a low shelf in the oven for the last 15–20 minutes of the birds' cooking time.

10 Serve the birds on a bed of dirty rice with the roasting juices (drained of fat) poured over.

Chicken Kiev

Cut through the crispy-coated chicken to reveal a creamy filling with just a hint of garlic.

INGREDIENTS

Serves 4

4 large chicken breasts, boned and
    skinned
15ml/1 tbsp lemon juice
115g/4oz/^{1}/2 cup ricotta cheese
1 garlic clove, crushed
30ml/2 tbsp chopped fresh parsley
1.5ml/^{1}/4 tsp freshly grated nutmeg
30ml/2 tbsp plain flour
pinch of cayenne pepper
1.5ml/^{1}/4 tsp salt
115g/4oz/2 cups fresh white breadcrumbs
2 egg whites, lightly beaten
creamed potatoes, French beans and
    grilled tomatoes, to serve

1 Preheat the oven to 200°C/
400°F/Gas 6. Place the chicken
breasts between two sheets of clear
film and gently beat with a rolling
pin until flattened. Sprinkle with
the lemon juice.

2 Mix the ricotta cheese with the
garlic, 15ml/1 tbsp of the
chopped parsley and the nutmeg.
Shape into four 5cm/2in long rolls.

3 Put one portion of the cheese
and herb mixture in the centre
of each chicken breast and fold the
meat over, tucking in the edges to
enclose the filling completely.

4 Secure the chicken with cocktail sticks pushed through the
centre of each. Mix together the
flour, cayenne pepper and salt and
use to dust the chicken.

5 Mix together the breadcrumbs
and remaining parsley. Dip the
chicken into the egg whites, then
coat with the breadcrumbs. Chill
for 30 minutes in the fridge, then
dip into the egg white and breadcrumbs for a second time.

6 Put the chicken on a non-stick
baking sheet. Bake in the preheated oven for 25 minutes or
until the coating is golden brown
and the chicken completely
cooked. Remove the cocktail sticks
and serve with creamed potatoes,
French beans and grilled tomatoes.

Poussins with Raisin and Walnut Stuffing

Port wine-soaked raisins, walnuts and mushrooms make an unusual stuffing for poussins.

INGREDIENTS

Serves 4

250ml/8fl oz/1 cup Port wine
50g/2oz/^{1}/3 cup raisins
15ml/1 tbsp walnut oil
75g/3oz mushrooms, minced
1 large celery stick, minced
1 small onion, chopped
salt and pepper
50g/2oz/1 cup fresh breadcrumbs
50g/2oz/^{1}/2 cup chopped walnuts
15ml/1 tbsp each chopped fresh basil and
    parsley, or 30ml/2 tbsp chopped parsley
2.5ml/^{1}/2 tsp dried thyme
75g/3oz/6 tbsp butter, melted
4 poussins

1 Preheat the oven to 180°C/ 350°F/Gas 4.

2 In a small bowl, combine the Port wine and raisins and leave to soak for about 20 minutes.

3 Meanwhile, heat the oil in a non-stick pan. Add the mushrooms, celery, onion and 1.5ml/^{1}/4 tsp salt and cook over a low heat until softened, about 8–10 minutes. Leave to cool.

4 Drain the raisins, reserving the Port. Combine the raisins, breadcrumbs, walnuts, basil, parsley and thyme in a bowl. Stir in the onion mixture and 50g/2oz/ 4 tbsp of the butter. Add 2.5ml/^{1}/2 tsp salt and pepper to taste.

5 Fill the cavity of each poussin with the stuffing. Do not pack down. Tie the legs together, to enclose the stuffing securely.

6 Brush the poussins with the remaining butter and place in a baking dish just large enough to hold the birds comfortably. Pour over the reserved Port wine.

7 Roast, basting occasionally, for about 1 hour. Test by piercing the thigh with a skewer; the juices should run clear. Serve immediately with some of the juices.

Oven "Fried" Chicken

The chicken in this dish is not fried but baked until crisp in the oven.

Serves 4

4 large chicken pieces

50g/2oz/$^1/_2$ cup flour

2.5ml/$^1/_2$ tsp salt

1.5ml/$^1/_4$ tsp pepper

1 egg

30ml/2 tbsp water

30ml/2 tbsp chopped mixed fresh herbs, such as parsley, basil and thyme

65g/2$^1/_2$ oz/1 cup dry breadcrumbs

25g/1oz/$^1/_3$ cup freshly grated Parmesan cheese

lemon wedges, for serving

1 Preheat the oven to 200°C/400°F/Gas 6.

2 Rinse the chicken in cold water. Pat dry with kitchen paper.

3 Combine the flour, salt and pepper on a plate and stir with a fork to mix. Coat the chicken pieces on all sides with the flour and shake off the excess.

4 Sprinkle a little water on to the chicken pieces, and coat again lightly with the seasoned flour.

5 Beat the egg with the water in a shallow dish. Stir in the herbs. Dip the chicken pieces into the egg mixture, turning them over to coat them thoroughly.

6 Combine the breadcrumbs and grated Parmesan cheese on a plate. Roll the chicken pieces in the crumbs, patting with your fingers to help them to adhere.

7 Place the chicken pieces in a greased shallow pan, large enough to hold them in one layer. Bake until thoroughly cooked and golden brown, 20–30 minutes. To check that they are cooked, prick with a fork; the juices that run out should be clear, not pink. Serve hot, with lemon wedges.

Blackened Chicken Breasts

*Chicken breasts with a seasoned
coating of herbs and spices.*

INGREDIENTS

Serves 6

6 medium chicken breasts,
    boned and skinned
75g/3oz/6 tbsp butter or margarine
5ml/1 tsp garlic purée
60ml/4 tbsp finely grated onion
5ml/1 tsp cayenne
10ml/2 tsp sweet paprika
7.5ml/1$^{1}/_{2}$ tsp salt
2.5ml/$^{1}/_{2}$ tsp white pepper
5ml/1 tsp black pepper
1.5ml/$^{1}/_{4}$ tsp ground cumin
5ml/1 tsp dried thyme leaves

1 Slice each chicken breast piece
in half horizontally. Flatten
them down slightly with the heel
of the hand.

2 Melt the butter or margarine in
a small saucepan together with
the garlic purée.

3 Combine all the remaining
ingredients in a shallow bowl
and stir well. Brush the chicken
pieces on both sides with melted
butter or margarine, then sprinkle
evenly with the seasoned mixture.

4 Heat a large heavy frying pan
over high heat until a drop of
water sprinkled on the surface
sizzles. This will take 5–8 minutes.

5 Drizzle 5ml/1 tsp of melted
butter on each chicken piece.
Place them in the pan in an even
layer, 2 or 3 at a time. Cook until
the underside begins to blacken,
2–3 minutes. Turn over and cook
2–3 minutes more. Serve hot.

Chicken Tonnato

This low-fat version of the Italian dish "vitello tonnato" is garnished with fine strips of red pepper instead of the traditional anchovy fillets.

INGREDIENTS

Serves 4

450g/1lb chicken breasts,
   boned and skinned
1 small onion, sliced
1 bay leaf
4 black peppercorns
350ml/12fl oz/1¹/₂ cups chicken stock
200g/7oz can tuna in brine, drained
75ml/5 tbsp reduced calorie mayonnaise
30ml/2 tbsp lemon juice
2 red peppers, seeded and thinly sliced
about 25 capers, drained
pinch of salt
mixed salad and tomatoes, to serve

4 Put the tuna, mayonnaise, lemon juice, 45ml/3 tbsp of the reduced stock and salt into a blender or food processor and purée until smooth.

5 Stir in enough of the remaining stock to reduce the sauce to the thickness of double cream. Spoon over the chicken.

6 Arrange the strips of red pepper in a lattice pattern over the chicken. Put a caper in the centre of each square. Chill in the fridge for 1 hour and serve with a fresh mixed salad and tomatoes.

1 Put the chicken breasts in a single layer in a large, heavy-based saucepan. Add the onion, bay leaf, peppercorns and stock. Bring to the boil and reduce the heat. Cover and simmer for about 12 minutes, or until tender.

2 Turn off the heat and leave the chicken to cool in the stock, then remove with a slotted spoon. Slice the breasts thickly and arrange on a serving plate.

3 Boil the stock until reduced to about 75ml/5 tbsp. Strain through a fine sieve and cool.

Chicken and Tomato Hot-pot

Versatile minced chicken is perfect for family meals. Here, it's turned into tasty meatballs.

INGREDIENTS

Serves 4

25g/1oz white bread, crust removed

30ml/2 tbsp milk

1 garlic clove, crushed

2.5ml/^{1}/2 tsp caraway seeds

225g/8oz/2 cups minced chicken

1 egg white

350ml/12fl oz/1^1/2 cups chicken stock

400g/14oz can plum tomatoes

15ml/1 tbsp tomato purée

90g/3^1/2oz/^{1}/2 cup easy-cook rice

salt and black pepper

15ml/1 tbsp chopped fresh basil,
   to garnish

carrot and courgette ribbons, to serve

4 Put the chicken stock, tomatoes and tomato purée into a large, heavy-based saucepan and bring to the boil.

5 Add the rice, stir and cook briskly for about 5 minutes. Turn the heat down to a simmer.

6 Meanwhile, shape the chicken mixture into 16 small balls. Carefully drop them into the tomato stock and simmer for a further 8–10 minutes, or until the chicken balls and rice are cooked. Garnish with the basil, and serve with carrot and courgette ribbons.

1 Cut the bread into small cubes and put into a mixing bowl. Sprinkle over the milk and leave to soak for 5 minutes.

2 Add the garlic clove, caraway seeds, chicken, salt and freshly ground black pepper to the bread. Mix together well.

3 Whisk the egg white until stiff, then fold, half at a time, into the chicken mixture. Chill for 10 minutes in the fridge.

Roast Chicken with Fennel

In Italy this dish is prepared with wild fennel. Cultivated fennel bulb works just as well.

Serves 4–5

1.6kg/3^1/2lb roasting chicken
1 onion, quartered
100ml/4fl oz/^{1}/2 cup olive oil
2 medium fennel bulbs
1 clove garlic, peeled
pinch of grated nutmeg
3–4 thin slices pancetta or bacon
100ml/4fl oz/^{1}/2 cup dry white wine
salt and black pepper

1 Preheat the oven to 180°C/ 350°F/Gas 4. Sprinkle the chicken cavity with salt and pepper. Place the onion quarters in the cavity. Rub the chicken with about 45ml/3 tbsp of the olive oil. Place in a roasting tin.

2 Cut the green fronds from the tops of the fennel bulbs. Chop the fronds together with the garlic. Place in a small bowl and mix with the nutmeg and seasoning.

3 Sprinkle the fennel mixture over the chicken, pressing it on to the oiled skin. Cover the breast with the slices of pancetta or bacon. Sprinkle with 30ml/2 tbsp of the oil. Place in the oven and roast for 30 minutes.

4 Meanwhile, boil or steam the fennel bulbs until barely tender. Remove from the heat and cut into quarters or sixths length-ways. After the chicken has been cooking for 30 minutes, remove the pan from the oven. Baste the chicken with any oils in the pan.

5 Arrange the fennel pieces around the chicken. Sprinkle the fennel with the remaining oil. Pour about half the wine over the chicken, and return to the oven.

6 After 30 minutes more, baste the chicken again. Pour on the remaining wine. Cook for 15–20 minutes. To test, prick the thigh with a fork. If the juices run clear, the chicken is cooked. Serve the chicken surrrounded by the fennel.

Chicken with Ham and Cheese

This tasty combination comes from Emilia-Romagna, where it is also prepared with veal.

Serves 4

4 small chicken breasts, skinned
    and boned
flour seasoned with salt and freshly
    ground black pepper, for dredging
50g/2oz/4 tbsp butter
3–4 leaves fresh sage
4 thin slices prosciutto crudo,
    or cooked ham, cut in half
50g/2oz/^{1}/2 cup freshly grated
    Parmesan cheese

1 Cut each breast in half length-ways to make two flat fillets of approximately the same thickness. Dredge the chicken in the seasoned flour, and shake off the excess.

2 Preheat the grill. Heat the butter in a large heavy frying pan and add the sage leaves. Add the chicken, in one layer, and cook over low to moderate heat until golden brown on both sides, turning as necessary. This will take about 15 minutes.

3 Remove the chicken from the heat, and arrange on a flame-proof serving dish or grill pan. Place one piece of ham on each chicken fillet and top with the grated Parmesan. Grill for 3–4 minutes, or until the cheese has melted. Serve at once.

Chicken Roll

The roll can be prepared and cooked the day before and will freeze well too. Remove from the fridge about an hour before serving.

Serves 8
2kg/4¹/₂lb chicken

For the stuffing
1 medium onion, finely chopped
50g/2oz/4 tbsp melted butter
350g/12oz/2 cups lean minced pork
115g/4oz streaky bacon, chopped
15ml/1 tbsp chopped fresh parsley
10ml/2 tsp chopped fresh thyme
115g/4oz/2 cups fresh white breadcrumbs
30ml/2 tbsp sherry
1 large egg, beaten
25g/1oz/¹/₄ cup shelled pistachio nuts
25g/1oz/¹/₄ cup stoned black olives
    (about 12)
salt and black pepper

1 To make the stuffing, cook the chopped onion gently in 25g/1oz/2 tbsp of the butter until soft. Turn into a bowl and cool. Add the remaining ingredients, mix thoroughly and season with salt and black pepper.

2 To bone the chicken, use a small, sharp knife to remove the wing tips. Turn the chicken on to its breast and cut a line down the backbone.

3 Cut the meat away from the carcass, scraping the bones clean. Carefully cut through the sinew around the leg and wing joints and scrape down the bones to free them. Remove the carcass, taking care not to cut through the skin along the breastbone.

4 To stuff the chicken, lay it flat, skin side down and flatten as much as possible. Shape the stuffing down the centre of the chicken and fold in the sides.

5 Sew the meat neatly together, using a needle and dark thread. Tie with fine string into a roll.

6 Preheat the oven to 180°C/ 350°F/Gas 4. Put the roll, join underneath, on a rack in a roasting tin and brush with the remaining butter. Cook, uncovered, for about 1¹/₄ hours. Baste with the juices during cooking. Leave to cool. Remove the string and thread. Wrap in foil and chill until needed.

Traditional Roast Chicken

Serve with bacon rolls, chipolata sausages, gravy and stuffing balls.

INGREDIENTS

Serves 4

1.75kg/4lb chicken
streaky bacon rashers
25g/1oz/2 tbsp butter
salt and black pepper

Prune and nut stuffing
25g/1oz/2 tbsp butter
50g/2oz/^{1}/2 cup chopped stoned
    prunes
50g/2oz/^{1}/2 cup chopped walnuts
50g/2oz/1 cup fresh breadcrumbs
1 egg, beaten
15ml/1 tbsp chopped fresh parsley
15ml/1 tbsp chopped fresh chives
30ml/2 tbsp sherry or Port

For the gravy
30ml/2 tbsp plain flour
300ml/^{1}/2 pint/1^1/4 cups chicken stock

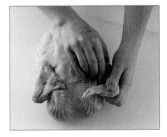

1 Preheat the oven to 190°C/ 375°F/Gas 5. Mix all the stuffing ingredients together in a bowl and season well.

2 Stuff the neck end of the chicken quite loosely, allowing room for the breadcrumbs to swell during cooking. (Any remaining stuffing can be shaped into balls and fried to accompany the roast.)

3 Tuck the neck skin under the bird to secure the stuffing and hold in place with the wing tips or sew with strong thread or fine string.

4 Place in a roasting tin and cover the breast with the bacon rashers. Spread with the remaining butter, cover loosely with foil and roast for about 1^1/2 hours. Baste with the juices in the roasting tin 3 or 4 times during cooking.

5 Remove any trussing string and transfer to a serving plate, cover with foil and leave to stand while making the gravy. (This standing time allows the flesh to relax and makes carving easier.)

6 Spoon off the fat from the juices in the roasting tin. Blend the flour into the juices and cook gently until golden brown. Add the stock, bring to the boil, stirring until thickened. Adjust the seasoning and strain into a jug to serve.

Roast Chicken with Celeriac

*Chicken with a stuffing of celeriac,
bacon, onion and herbs.*

Serves 4

1.6kg/3^1/2lb chicken
15g/^{1}/2oz/1 tbsp butter

For the stuffing

450g/1lb celeriac, chopped
25g/1oz/2 tbsp butter
3 slices bacon, chopped
1 onion, finely chopped
leaves from 1 thyme sprig, chopped
leaves from 1 small tarragon
    sprig, chopped
30ml/2 tbsp chopped fresh parsley
75g/3oz/1^1/2 cups fresh brown
    breadcrumbs
dash of Worcestershire sauce
1 egg
salt and pepper

1 To make the stuffing, cook the
celeriac in boiling water until
tender. Drain well and chop finely.

2 Heat the butter in a saucepan,
then gently cook the bacon and
onion until the onion is soft. Stir
the celeriac and herbs into the pan
and cook, stirring occasionally, for
2–3 minutes. Meanwhile, preheat
the oven to 200°C/400°F/Gas 6.

3 Remove the pan from the heat
and stir in the fresh breadcrumbs, Worcestershire sauce,
seasoning and sufficient egg to
bind.

4 Place the stuffing in the neck
end of the chicken. Season the
bird's skin, then rub with the
butter. Roast the chicken, basting
occasionally with the juices, for
1^1/4–1^1/2 hours, until the juices run
clear when the thickest part of the
leg is pierced. Rest for 10 minutes
in a warm place before carving.

Poussins with Grapes in Vermouth

A rather special dish which is ideal to serve when entertaining.

INGREDIENTS

Serves 4

4 oven-ready poussins, about
   450g/1lb each
50g/2oz/4 tbsp butter, softened
2 shallots, chopped
60ml/4 tbsp chopped fresh parsley
225g/8oz white grapes, preferably
   muscatel, halved and seeded
150ml/¼ pint/⅔ cup white vermouth
5ml/1 tsp cornflour
60ml/4 tbsp double cream
30ml/2 tbsp pine nuts, toasted
salt and black pepper
watercress sprigs, to garnish

1 Preheat the oven to 200°C/
400°F/Gas 6. Spread the softened butter all over the poussins
and put a hazelnut-sized piece in
the cavity of each bird.

2 Mix together the shallots and
parsley and place a quarter of
the mixture inside each poussin.
Put the poussins side by side in a
large roasting tin and roast for
40–50 minutes, or until the juices
run clear when the thickest part of
the flesh is pierced with a skewer.
Put the poussins on to a warm
serving dish, cover and keep warm.

3 Skim off most of the fat from
the roasting tin, then add the
grapes and vermouth. Place the tin
directly over a low flame for a few
minutes to warm and slightly
soften the grapes.

4 Lift the grapes out of the tin
using a slotted spoon and
scatter them around the poussins.
Keep covered. Stir the cornflour
into the cream, then add to the pan
juices. Cook gently for a few
minutes, stirring, until the sauce
has thickened. Adjust seasoning.

5 Pour the sauce around the
poussins. Sprinkle with the
toasted pine nuts and garnish with
watercress sprigs.

Stir-fried Chicken with Mange-touts

Juicy chicken stir-fried with mange-touts, cashews and water chestnuts.

INGREDIENTS

Serves 4

30ml/2 tbsp sesame oil

90ml/6 tbsp lemon juice

1 garlic clove, crushed

1cm/^{1}/$_2$ in piece fresh root ginger, peeled and grated

5ml/1 tsp clear honey

450g/1lb chicken breast fillets, cut into strips

115g/4oz mange-touts, trimmed

30ml/2 tbsp groundnut oil

50g/2oz/^{1}/$_2$ cup cashew nuts

6 spring onions, cut into strips

225g/8oz can water chestnuts, drained and thinly sliced

salt

saffron rice, to serve

1 Mix together the sesame oil, lemon juice, garlic, ginger and honey in a shallow non-metallic dish. Add the chicken and mix well. Cover and leave to marinate for at least 3–4 hours.

2 Blanch the mange-touts in boiling salted water for 1 minute. Drain and refresh under cold running water.

3 Drain the chicken strips and reserve the marinade. Heat the groundnut oil in a wok or large frying pan, add the cashew nuts and stir-fry for about 1–2 minutes until golden brown. Remove the cashew nuts from the wok or frying pan using a slotted spoon and set aside.

4 Add the chicken and stir-fry for 3–4 minutes, until golden brown. Add the spring onions, mange-touts, water chestnuts and the reserved marinade. Cook for a few minutes, until the chicken is tender and the sauce is bubbling and hot. Stir in the cashew nuts and serve with saffron rice.

Stuffed Chicken Breasts with Cream Sauce

Chicken breasts filled with a leek and lime-flavoured stuffing and served in a cream sauce.

INGREDIENTS

Serves 4

4 large chicken breasts,
   boned and skinned
50g/2oz/4 tbsp butter
3 large leeks, white and pale green
   parts only, thinly sliced
5ml/1 tsp grated lime zest
250ml/8fl oz/1 cup chicken stock or half
   stock and half dry white wine
120ml/4fl oz/^{1}/$_2$ cup whipping or
   double cream
15ml/1 tbsp lime juice
salt and pepper

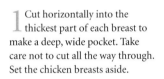

1 Cut horizontally into the thickest part of each breast to make a deep, wide pocket. Take care not to cut all the way through. Set the chicken breasts aside.

2 Melt half the butter in a large heavy frying pan over low heat. Add the leeks and lime zest and cook, stirring occasionally, for 15–20 minutes or until the leeks are very soft but not coloured.

3 Turn the leeks into a bowl and season to taste with salt and pepper. Leave to cool. Wash and dry the frying pan.

4 Divide the leeks among the chicken breasts, packing the pockets full. Secure the openings with wooden cocktail sticks.

5 Melt the remaining butter in the frying pan over moderately high heat. Add the stuffed breasts and brown lightly on both sides.

6 Add the stock and bring to the boil. Cover and simmer for about 10 minutes or until the chicken is cooked through. Carefully turn the breasts over halfway through the cooking.

7 With a slotted spatula, remove the breasts from the pan and keep warm. Boil the cooking liquid until it is reduced by half.

8 Stir the cream into the cooking liquid and boil until reduced by about half again. Stir in the lime juice and season to taste.

9 Remove the cocktail sticks from the breasts. Cut each breast on the diagonal into 1cm/^{1}/$_2$ in slices, pour the sauce over them and serve.

VARIATION

For Onion-stuffed Chicken Breasts, use 2 sweet onions, halved and thinly sliced, instead of leeks.

Pasta with Chicken Livers

*Chicken livers in a piquant sauce
served with pasta.*

INGREDIENTS

Serves 4

225g/8oz chicken livers, defrosted
    if frozen
30ml/2 tbsp olive oil
2 garlic cloves, crushed
175g/6oz rindless smoked back bacon,
    roughly chopped
400g/14oz can chopped tomatoes
150ml/¼ pint/⅔ cup chicken stock
15ml/1 tbsp tomato purée
15ml/1 tbsp dry sherry
30ml/2 tbsp chopped mixed fresh herbs,
    such as parsley, rosemary and basil
350g/12oz dried orecchiette pasta
salt and black pepper
freshly grated Parmesan cheese, to serve

1 Wash and trim the chicken
livers. Cut into bite-sized
pieces. Heat the oil in a sauté pan
and fry the chicken livers for 3–4
minutes until tender.

2 Add the garlic and bacon to the
pan and fry until golden
brown. Add the tomatoes, chicken
stock, tomato purée, sherry, herbs
and seasoning to taste.

3 Bring the sauce to the boil and
simmer gently, uncovered, for
about 5 minutes until the sauce
has thickened. Stir from time
to time.

4 Meanwhile, cook the pasta in
boiling salted water for about
12 minutes until "al dente". Drain,
then toss into the sauce. Serve hot,
sprinkled with Parmesan cheese.

Chicken Baked in a Salt Crust

*This unusual dish is extremely easy
to make. Once it is cooked, you just
break away the salt crust to reveal
the wonderfully tender, golden
brown chicken underneath.*

INGREDIENTS

Serves 4

1.5kg/3–3½ lb corn-fed oven-ready
    chicken
bunch of mixed fresh herbs, such as
    rosemary, thyme, marjoram and parsley
about 1.5kg/3–3½ lb/7 cups coarse sea
    salt
1 egg white
1–2 whole heads of baked garlic, to serve

1 Preheat the oven to 180°C/
350°F/Gas 4. Wipe the chicken.
Put the herbs into the cavity, then
truss the chicken.

2 Mix together the sea salt and
egg white until all the salt
crystals are moistened. Select a
roasting tin into which the chicken
will fit neatly, then line it with a
large double layer of foil.

3 Spread a thick layer of the salt
in the foil-lined tin and put the
chicken on top. Cover with the
remaining salt and shape neatly,
around the chicken, making sure it
is completely enclosed.

4 Bring the foil edges up and
over the chicken to enclose it
and bake in the oven for 1½ hours.
Remove from the oven and leave to
rest for 10 minutes.

5 Carefully lift the foil package
from the container and open.
Break the salt crust and brush any
traces of salt from the bird. Serve
with baked whole heads of garlic.
Slip each clove from its skin and
eat with a bite of chicken.

Risotto with Chicken

This is a complete meal cooked conveniently all in one pan.

INGREDIENTS

Serves 4

2 tablespoons olive oil

8oz/225g chicken breast, skinned, boned
   and cut into 2.5cm/1in cubes

1 onion, finely chopped

1 garlic clove, finely chopped

1.5ml/^{1}/$_4$ tsp saffron strands

50g/2oz/^{1}/$_2$ cup Parma ham, cut
   into thin strips

450g/1lb/2 cups risotto rice,
   preferably Arborio

120ml/4fl oz/^{1}/$_2$ cup dry white wine

1.75 litres/3 pints/7^1/$_2$ cups simmering
   chicken stock

25g/1oz/2 tbsp butter (optional)

25g/1oz/^{1}/$_3$ cup freshly grated Parmesan
   cheese, plus more to serve

salt and pepper

1 Heat the oil in a wide heavy-based pan over moderately high heat. Add the chicken cubes and cook, stirring, until they start to turn white.

2 Reduce the heat to low. Add the onion, garlic, saffron and Parma ham. Cook, stirring, until the onion is soft. Stir in the risotto rice and mix well. Sauté for 1–2 minutes, stirring constantly.

3 Add the wine and bring to the boil. Simmer gently until almost all the wine is absorbed.

4 Add the simmering stock, a ladleful at a time, and cook until the rice is just tender and the risotto creamy.

5 Add the butter, if using, and Parmesan cheese and stir in well. Season with salt and pepper to taste. Serve the risotto hot, sprinkled with more Parmesan.

Cannelloni al Forno

A lighter alternative to the usual beef-filled, béchamel-coated version. Fill with ricotta, onion and mushroom for a vegetarian recipe.

INGREDIENTS

Serves 4–6

450g/1lb/4 cups skinned and boned
   chicken breast, cooked

225g/8oz mushrooms

2 garlic cloves, crushed

30ml/2 tbsp chopped fresh parsley

15ml/1 tbsp chopped fresh tarragon

1 egg, beaten

fresh lemon juice

12–18 cannelloni tubes

475ml/16 fl oz/2 cups ready-made tomato
   sauce

50g/2oz/^{2}/3 cup freshly grated Parmesan
   cheese

salt and pepper

1 sprig fresh parsley, to garnish

1 Preheat the oven to 200°C/
400°F/Gas 6. Place the chicken in a blender or food processor and blend until finely minced. Transfer to a bowl.

2 Place the mushrooms, garlic, parsley and tarragon in the food processor and blend until finely minced.

3 Beat the mushroom mixture into the chicken mixture thoroughly, then add the egg, salt and pepper and lemon juice to taste and mix together well.

4 If necessary, cook the cannelloni in plenty of salted boiling water according to the instructions, then drain well on a clean dish towel.

5 Place the filling in a piping bag fitted with a large plain nozzle. Use this to fill each tube of cannelloni once they are cool enough to handle.

6 Lay the filled cannelloni tightly together in a single layer in a buttered shallow ovenproof dish. Spoon over the tomato sauce and sprinkle with Parmesan cheese. Bake in the oven for 30 minutes or until brown and bubbling. Serve garnished with a sprig of parsley.

Chicken and Curry Mayonnaise Sandwich

A very useful and appetizing way of using leftover pieces of chicken.

Serves 2

4 slices Granary bread

25g/1oz/2 tbsp softened butter

115g/4oz cooked chicken, sliced

45ml/3 tbsp Curry Mayonnaise

1 bunch watercress, trimmed

1 Spread the bread with butter and arrange the chicken over two of the slices.

2 Spread the Curry Mayonnaise over the chicken slices.

3 Arrange a few sprigs of watercress on top, cover with the remaining bread, press lightly together and cut in half.

CURRY MAYONNAISE

Makes about 150ml/5fl oz/²/₃ cup

120ml/4fl oz/^{1}/2 cup mayonnaise

10ml/2 tsp concentrated curry sauce

2.5ml/^{1}/2 tsp lemon juice

10ml/2 tsp sieved apricot jam

Mix all the ingredients together thoroughly and chill until needed.

Oriental Chicken Sandwich

*This filling is also good served in
warmed pitta bread, in which case
cut the chicken into small cubes
before marinating. Grill on skewers
and serve warm.*

INGREDIENTS

Serves 2

15ml/1 tbsp soy sauce
5ml/1 tsp clear honey
5ml/1 tsp sesame oil
1 garlic clove, crushed
175g/6oz chicken breast,
    boned and skinned
4 slices white bread
60ml/4 tbsp peanut butter
25g/1oz/2 tbsp beansprouts
25g/1oz red pepper, seeded
    and finely sliced
2 sprigs parsley, to garnish

1 Mix together the soy sauce,
honey, sesame oil and garlic.
Brush over the chicken breast.

2 Grill the chicken for 3–4
minutes on each side until
cooked through, then slice thinly.

3 Spread two slices of the bread
with some of the peanut butter.

4 Arrange the slices of chicken
on top of the peanut butter.

5 Spread a little more peanut
butter over the chicken.

6 Sprinkle over the beansprouts
and red pepper and sandwich
together with the remaining slices
of bread. Cut in half, if desired.

Chicken and Shiitake Mushroom Pizza

The addition of shiitake mushrooms adds an earthy flavour to this colourful pizza, while fresh red chilli gives a hint of spiciness.

Serves 3–4

45ml/3 tbsp olive oil
350g/12oz/3 cups chicken breast fillets, skinned and cut into thin strips
1 bunch spring onions, sliced
1 fresh red chilli, seeded and chopped
1 red pepper, seeded and cut into thin strips
75g/3oz fresh shiitake mushrooms, wiped and sliced
45–60ml/3–4 tbsp chopped fresh coriander
1 pizza base, about 25–30cm/10–12in diameter
15ml/1 tbsp chilli oil
150g/5oz/11/4 cups mozzarella cheese
salt and black pepper

1 Preheat the oven to 220°C/425°F/Gas 7. Heat 30ml/2tbsp of the olive oil in a wok or large frying pan. Add the chicken, spring onions, chilli, pepper and mushrooms and stir-fry over a high heat for 2–3 minutes until the chicken is firm but still slightly pink within. Season.

2 Pour off any excess oil, then set aside the chicken mixture until cool.

3 Stir the fresh coriander into the chicken mixture.

4 Brush the pizza base with the chilli oil.

5 Spoon over the chicken mixture and drizzle over the remaining olive oil.

6 Grate the mozzarella and sprinkle over. Bake for 15–20 minutes until crisp and golden. Serve immediately.

Smoked Chicken Pizza

These ingredients complement each other perfectly and make a really delicious topping.

INGREDIENTS

Serves 4

4 small pizza bases, about 13cm/
    5in diameter
45ml/3 tbsp olive oil
60ml/4 tbsp sun-dried tomato paste
2 yellow peppers, seeded and cut
    into thin strips
175g/6oz sliced smoked chicken
    or turkey, chopped
150g/5oz/1¹/4 cups mozzarella cheese,
    cubed
30ml/2 tbsp chopped fresh basil
salt and black pepper

1 Preheat the oven to 220°C/
425°F/Gas 7. Place the pizza
bases well apart on two greased
baking sheets.

2 Brush the pizza bases with
15ml/1 tbsp of the oil, then
brush generously with tomato
paste.

3 Stir-fry the peppers in half the
remaining oil for 3–4 minutes.

4 Arrange the chicken and
peppers on top of the sun-
dried tomato paste.

5 Scatter over the mozzarella and
basil. Season to taste with salt
and black pepper.

6 Drizzle over the remaining oil
and bake in the oven for
15–20 minutes until crisp and
golden. Serve immediately.

Chicken and Avocado Pitta Pizzas

Pitta bread is used here to make quick bases for a tasty pizza.

INGREDIENTS

Serves 4

8 plum tomatoes, quartered

45–60ml/3–4 tbsp olive oil

1 large ripe avocado

8 pitta bread rounds

6–7 slices of cooked chicken, chopped

1 onion, thinly sliced

275g/10oz/2^1/2 cups grated Cheddar cheese

30ml/2 tbsp chopped fresh coriander

salt and pepper

1 Preheat the oven to 230°C/ 450°F/Gas 8.

2 Place the tomatoes in a baking dish. Drizzle over 15ml/1 tbsp of the oil and season to taste. Bake for 30 minutes; do not stir.

3 Remove the baking dish from the oven and mash the tomatoes with a fork, removing the skins as you mash. Set aside.

4 Peel and stone the avocado. Cut into 16 thin slices.

5 Brush the edges of the pitta breads with oil. Arrange the breads on two baking sheets.

6 Spread each pitta with mashed tomato, almost to the edges.

7 Top each with 2 avocado slices. Sprinkle with the chicken, then add a few onion slices. Season to taste. Sprinkle on the cheese.

8 Place one sheet in the middle of the oven and bake until the cheese begins to melt, about 15–20 minutes. Sprinkle with half the coriander and serve. Meanwhile, bake the second batch of pizzas, cook and serve them hot.

Chicken Breasts with Tomato-corn Salsa

This hot tomato salsa is good with any grilled or barbecued meats.

INGREDIENTS

Serves 4

4 chicken breast halves, about 175g/6oz
    each, boned and skinned
30ml/2 tbsp fresh lemon juice
30ml/2 tbsp olive oil
10ml/2 tsp ground cumin
10ml/2 tsp dried oregano
15ml/1 tbsp coarse black pepper
salt

For the salsa
1 fresh hot green chilli pepper
450g/1lb tomatoes, seeded and chopped
250g/9oz/1¹/4 cups sweetcorn, freshly
    cooked or thawed frozen
3 spring onions, chopped
15ml/1 tbsp chopped fresh parsley
30ml/2 tbsp chopped fresh coriander
30ml/2 tbsp fresh lemon juice
45ml/3 tbsp olive oil
5ml/1 tsp salt

1 With a meat mallet, pound the chicken breasts between two sheets of clear film until thin.

2 In a shallow dish, combine the lemon juice, oil, cumin, oregano and pepper.

3 Add the chicken and turn to coat. Cover and leave to stand for at least 2 hours, or chill overnight.

4 To make the salsa, char the chilli skin either over a gas flame or under the grill. Leave to cool for 5 minutes. Wearing rubber gloves, carefully rub off the charred skin. For a less hot flavour, discard the seeds.

5 Chop the chilli very finely and place in a bowl. Add the remaining salsa ingredients and mix well.

6 Remove the chicken from the marinade. Season lightly.

7 Heat a ridged grill pan. Add the chicken breasts and cook until browned, about 3 minutes. Turn and cook for 3–4 minutes more. Serve with the chilli salsa.

Pan-fried Honey Chicken Drumsticks

*The sweetness of the honey contrasts
well with the lemon and soy sauce.*

INGREDIENTS

Serves 4

115g/4oz/¹/₂ cup clear honey

juice of 1 lemon

30ml/2 tbsp soy sauce

15ml/1 tbsp sesame seeds

2.5ml/¹/₂ tsp fresh or dried thyme leaves

12 chicken drumsticks

2.5ml/¹/₂ tsp salt

2.5ml/¹/₂ tsp pepper

80g/3¹/₄ oz/³/₄ cup flour

45ml/3 tbsp butter or margarine

45ml/3 tbsp vegetable oil

120ml/4fl oz/¹/₂ cup white wine

120ml/4fl oz/¹/₂ cup chicken stock

1 In a large bowl, combine the
honey, lemon juice, soy sauce,
sesame seeds and thyme. Add the
chicken drumsticks and mix to
coat them well. Leave to marinate
in a cool place for 2 hours or more,
turning occasionally.

2 Mix the salt, pepper and flour
in a shallow bowl. Drain the
drumsticks, reserving the
marinade. Roll them in the
seasoned flour to coat all over.

3 Heat the butter or margarine
with the oil in a large frying
pan. When hot and sizzling, add
the drumsticks. Brown them on all
sides. Reduce the heat to medium–
low and cook until the chicken is
done, 12–15 minutes.

4 Test the drumsticks with a
fork; the juices should be clear.
Remove the drumsticks to a
serving platter and keep hot.

5 Pour off most of the fat from
the pan. Add the wine, stock
and reserved marinade and stir
well to mix in the cooking juices
on the bottom of the pan. Bring to
the boil and simmer until reduced
by half. Check and adjust the
seasoning, then spoon the sauce
over the drumsticks and serve.

Chicken Liver Stir-fry

The final sprinkling of lemon, parsley and garlic gives this dish a delightfully fresh flavour and a wonderful aroma.

INGREDIENTS

Serves 4

500g/1¹/₄ lb chicken livers
75g/3oz/6 tbsp butter
175g/6oz field mushrooms
50g/2oz chanterelle mushrooms
3 cloves garlic, finely chopped
2 shallots, finely chopped
150ml/¹/₄ pint/²/₃ cup medium sherry
3 fresh rosemary sprigs
grated rind of 1 lemon
30ml/2 tbsp chopped fresh parsley
salt and black pepper
rosemary sprigs, to garnish
4 thick slices of white toast, to serve

1 Clean and trim the chicken livers to remove any gristle or muscle or discoloured bits.

2 Season the chicken livers generously with salt and ground black pepper, tossing well to coat them all thoroughly.

3 Heat a wok or frying pan and add 15g/¹/₂oz/1 tbsp of the butter. When melted, add the livers in batches (melting more butter when necessary but reserving 25g/1oz/2 tbsp for the vegetables) and flash-fry until golden brown. Drain using a slotted spoon and transfer to a plate, then place in a low oven to keep warm.

4 Cut the field mushrooms into thick slices. If large, cut the chanterelles in half.

5 Heat the wok and add the remaining butter. Stir in two-thirds of the chopped garlic and the shallots and stir-fry for 1 minute until golden brown. Stir in the mushrooms and continue to cook for a further 2 minutes.

6 Add the sherry, bring to the boil and simmer for 2–3 minutes until syrupy. Add the rosemary, seasoning and livers to the pan. Stir-fry for 1 minute. Garnish with the rosemary, and sprinkle with a mixture of lemon, parsley and remaining chopped garlic. Serve with slices of toast.

ONE POT MEALS

Nasi Goreng

This dish is originally from Thailand, but can easily be adapted by adding any cooked ingredients you have to hand. Crispy prawn crackers make an ideal accompaniment.

Serves 4

225g/8oz/1 cup long grain rice

2 eggs

30ml/2 tbsp vegetable oil

1 green chilli

2 spring onions, roughly chopped

2 cloves garlic, crushed

225g/8oz cooked chicken

225g/8oz cooked prawns

45ml/3 tbsp dark soy sauce

prawn crackers, to serve

1 Rinse the rice and then cook for 10–12 minutes in 475ml/16fl oz/2 cups water in a pan with a tight-fitting lid. When cooked, refresh under cold water.

2 Lightly beat the eggs. Heat 15ml/1 tbsp of oil in a small frying pan and swirl in the beaten egg. When cooked on one side, flip over and cook on the other side. Remove from the pan and leave to cool. Cut the omelette into strips.

3 Carefully remove the seeds from the chilli and chop finely, wearing rubber gloves to protect your hands if necessary. Place the spring onions, chilli and garlic in a blender or food processor and blend to a paste.

4 Heat the wok, and then add the remaining oil. When the oil is hot, add the chilli paste and stir-fry for 1 minute.

5 Stir the chicken and prawns into the chilli paste.

6 Add the rice and stir-fry for 3–4 minutes. Stir in the soy sauce and serve with prawn crackers.

Chicken and Rice Vermicelli

*This delicious dish makes a filling
meal. Take care when frying vermicelli as it has a tendency to spit
when added to hot oil.*

INGREDIENTS

Serves 4

120ml/4fl oz/^{1}/$_2$ cup vegetable oil

225g/8oz rice vermicelli

150g/5oz French beans, topped, tailed and
 halved lengthways

1 onion, finely chopped

2 chicken breasts, about 175g/6oz each,
 boned, skinned and cut into strips

5ml/1 tsp chilli powder

225g/8oz cooked prawns

45ml/3 tbsp dark soy sauce

45ml/3 tbsp white wine vinegar

10ml/2 tsp caster sugar

fresh coriander sprigs, to garnish

1 Heat a wok or frying pan, then
add 60ml/4 tbsp of the oil.
Break up the vermicelli into 7.5cm/
3in lengths. When the oil is hot, fry
the vermicelli in batches. Remove
from the heat and keep warm.

2 Heat the remaining oil, then
add the French beans, chopped
onion and chicken and stir-fry
together for 3 minutes, until the
chicken strips are cooked.

3 Sprinkle in the chilli powder.
Stir in the cooked prawns, soy
sauce, vinegar and sugar, and stir-
fry for 2 minutes.

4 Serve the chicken, prawns and
vegetables on the fried
vermicelli, garnished with sprigs
of fresh coriander.

Italian Chicken

Sun-dried tomatoes and pesto are a winning combination in this dish.

Serves 4

30ml/2 tbsp plain flour
4 chicken portions (legs, breasts or
   quarters), skinned
30ml/2 tbsp olive oil
1 onion, chopped
2 garlic cloves, chopped
1 red pepper, seeded and chopped
400g/14oz can chopped tomatoes
30ml/2 tbsp red pesto sauce
4 sun-dried tomatoes in oil, chopped
150ml/¼ pint/⅔ cup chicken stock
5ml/1 tsp dried oregano
8 black olives, stoned
salt and black pepper
chopped fresh basil and a few basil leaves,
   to garnish
tagliatelle, to serve

1 Place the flour and seasoning in a plastic bag. Add the chicken pieces and shake well until coated. Heat the oil in a flame-proof casserole, add the chicken and brown quickly. Remove with a spoon and set aside.

2 Lower the heat and add the onion, garlic and red pepper and cook for 5 minutes.

3 Stir in the remaining ingredients, except olives and bring to the boil. Return the sautéed chicken portions to the casserole, season lightly, cover and simmer for 30–35 minutes, or until the chicken is cooked.

4 Add the olives and simmer for a further 5 minutes. Transfer to a warmed serving dish, sprinkle with the chopped fresh basil and garnish with a few basil leaves.

Honey and Orange Glazed Chicken

This way of cooking chicken breasts is popular in America, Australia and Great Britain. It is ideal for an easy evening meal served with baked potatoes and salad.

Serves 4

4 x 175g/6oz boneless chicken breasts
15ml/1 tbsp oil
4 spring onions, chopped
1 garlic clove, crushed
45ml/3 tbsp clear honey
60ml/4 tbsp fresh orange juice
1 orange, peeled and segmented
30ml/2 tbsp soy sauce
fresh lemon balm or flat leaf parsley, to
   garnish
baked potatoes and mixed salad, to serve

1 Preheat the oven to 190°C/ 375°F/Gas 5. Place the chicken breasts in a shallow roasting tin and set aside.

2 Heat the oil in a small pan, and fry the spring onions and garlic for 2 minutes until softened. Add the clear honey, orange juice, orange segments and soy sauce to the pan, stirring well until the honey has dissolved.

3 Pour over the chicken and bake, uncovered, for about 45 minutes, basting with the honey glaze once or twice until the chicken is cooked. Garnish with the lemon balm or parsley and serve the chicken and its sauce with baked potatoes and a salad.

Louisiana Rice

A tasty meal of pork, rice, chicken livers and an array of spices.

Serves 4

60ml/4 tbsp vegetable oil
1 small aubergine, diced
225g/8oz minced pork
1 green pepper, seeded and chopped
2 sticks celery, chopped
1 onion, chopped
1 garlic clove, crushed
5ml/1 tsp cayenne pepper
5ml/1 tsp paprika
5ml/1 tsp black pepper
2.5ml/^{1}/$_2$ tsp salt
5ml/1 tsp dried thyme
2.5ml/^{1}/$_2$ tsp dried oregano
475ml/16fl oz/2 cups chicken stock
225g/8oz chicken livers, minced
150g/5oz/^{3}/$_4$ cup long grain rice
1 bay leaf
45ml/3 tbsp chopped fresh parsley
celery leaves, to garnish

1 Heat the oil in a frying pan until really hot, then add the diced aubergine and stir-fry for about 5 minutes.

2 Add the pork and cook for about 6–8 minutes, until browned, using a wooden spoon to break any lumps.

3 Add the chopped green pepper, celery, onion, garlic and all the spices and herbs. Cover and cook on a high heat for 5–6 minutes, stirring frequently from the bottom to scrape up and distribute the crispy brown bits.

4 Pour on the chicken stock and stir to clean the bottom of the pan. Cover and cook for 6 minutes over a moderate heat. Stir in the chicken livers, cook for 2 minutes, then stir in the rice and add the bay leaf.

5 Reduce the heat, cover and simmer for about 6–7 minutes. Turn off the heat and leave to stand for a further 10–15 minutes until the rice is tender. Remove the bay leaf and stir in the chopped parsley. Serve the rice hot, garnished with the celery leaves.

Chinese Special Fried Rice

Cooked white rice fried with a selection of other ingredients is a staple Chinese dish. This recipe combines a mixture of chicken, shrimps and vegetables with fried rice.

Serves 4

175g/6oz/1 cup long grain white rice
45ml/3 tbsp groundnut oil
1 garlic clove, crushed
4 spring onions, finely chopped
115g/4oz/1 cup diced cooked chicken
115g/4oz/1 cup cooked peeled shrimps
   (rinsed if canned)
50g/2oz/$^{1}/_{2}$ cup frozen peas
1 egg, beaten with a pinch of salt
50g/2oz/1 cup shredded lettuce
30ml/2 tbsp light soy sauce
pinch of caster sugar
salt and black pepper
15ml/1 tbsp chopped roasted cashew nuts,
   to garnish

1 Rinse the long grain rice in two to three changes of warm water to wash away some of the starch. Drain well.

2 Put the rice in a saucepan and add 15ml/1 tbsp of the oil and 350ml/12fl oz/1$^{1}/_{2}$ cups of water. Cover and bring to the boil, stir once, then cover and simmer for 12–15 minutes, until nearly all the water has been absorbed. Turn off the heat and leave covered for 10 minutes. Fluff up with a fork and leave to cool.

3 Heat the remaining oil in a wok or frying pan, add the garlic and spring onions and stir-fry for 30 seconds.

4 Add the chicken, shrimps and peas and stir-fry for 1–2 minutes, then add the cooked rice and stir-fry for a further 2 minutes. Pour in the egg and stir-fry until just set. Stir in the lettuce, soy sauce, sugar and seasoning.

5 Transfer to a warmed serving bowl, sprinkle with the chopped roasted cashew nuts and serve immediately.

Chicken Teriyaki

Boiled rice is the ideal accompaniment to this Japanese-style dish.

INGREDIENTS

Serves 4

450g/1lb chicken breasts, boned and
   skinned
orange segments and mustard and cress,
   to garnish

For the marinade
5ml/1 tsp sugar
15ml/1 tbsp rice wine
15ml/1 tbsp dry sherry
30ml/2 tbsp dark soy sauce
rind of 1 orange, grated

1 Finely slice the chicken breasts to give thin strips. Mix all the marinade ingredients together in a bowl.

2 Place the chicken in a bowl, pour over the marinade and leave to marinate for 15 minutes.

3 Heat a wok or large frying pan, add the chicken and marinade and stir-fry for 4–5 minutes. Serve the chicken garnished with orange segments and mustard and cress.

COOK'S TIP

Make sure the marinade is brought to the boil and cooked for 4–5 minutes, because it has been in contact with raw chicken.

Thai Fried Noodles

Pork, chicken and fish stir-fried with noodles and lime juice.

INGREDIENTS

Serves 4

225g/8oz thread egg noodles
60ml/4 tbsp vegetable oil
2 garlic cloves, finely chopped
175g/6oz pork tenderloin, sliced into thin strips
1 chicken breast (about 175g/6oz), boned, skinned and sliced into thin strips
115g/4oz/1 cup cooked peeled shrimps (rinsed if canned)
45ml/3 tbsp lime or lemon juice
45ml/3 tbsp oriental fish sauce
30ml/2 tbsp soft light brown sugar
2 eggs, beaten
$^1/_2$ red chilli, seeded and finely chopped
50g/2oz/$^1/_4$ cup beansprouts
60ml/4 tbsp roasted peanuts, chopped
3 spring onions, cut into 5cm/2in lengths and shredded
45ml/3 tbsp chopped fresh coriander

1 Place the noodles in a large pan of boiling water and leave to stand for about 5 minutes.

2 Meanwhile, heat 45ml/3 tbsp of the oil in a wok or large frying pan, add the garlic and cook for 30 seconds. Add the pork and chicken and stir-fry on a high heat until lightly browned, then add the shrimps and stir-fry for 2 minutes.

3 Add the lime or lemon juice, fish sauce and sugar and stir-fry until the sugar has dissolved.

4 Drain the noodles and add to the pan with the remaining 15ml/1 tbsp oil. Toss all the ingredients together.

5 Pour on the beaten eggs. Stir-fry until almost set, then add the chilli and beansprouts. Divide the peanuts, spring onions and coriander leaves into two and add half to the pan. Stir-fry for 2 minutes, then tip on to a serving platter. Sprinkle on the remaining peanuts, spring onions and coriander and serve at once.

Chicken and Prawn Jambalaya

The mixture of chicken, seafood and rice suggests a close relationship to the Spanish paella, but the name is more probably derived from jambon (the French for ham), à la ya (Creole for rice). Jambalayas are a colourful mixture of highly flavoured ingredients, and are always made in large quantities for big family or celebration meals.

INGREDIENTS

Serves 10

2 x 1.5kg/3lb chickens

450g/1lb piece raw smoked gammon

50g/2oz/4 tbsp lard or bacon fat

50g/2oz/^{1}/2 cup plain flour

3 medium onions, finely sliced

2 green peppers, seeded and sliced

675g/1^1/2lb tomatoes, skinned and chopped

2–3 garlic cloves, crushed

10ml/2 tsp chopped fresh thyme or 5ml/ 1 tsp dried thyme

24 cooked Mediterranean prawns, heads removed and peeled

500g/1^1/4lb/3 cups American long-grain rice

2–3 dashes Tabasco sauce

1 bunch spring onions, finely chopped (including the green parts)

45ml/3 tbsp chopped fresh parsley

salt and black pepper

COOK'S TIP

The roux thickening is a vital part of Cajun cooking, particularly essential to jambalaya. Cook the roux over a low heat, watching like a hawk to see it doesn't develop dark flecks, which indicate burning. Don't stop stirring, for an instant.

1 Cut each chicken into 10 pieces and season to taste with salt and pepper.

2 Dice the gammon, discarding the rind and fat.

3 In a large heavy-based pan melt the lard or bacon fat and brown the chicken pieces all over, lifting them out with a slotted spoon and setting them aside as they are done.

4 Turn the heat down, sprinkle the flour on to the fat in the pan and stir continuously until the roux turns light golden brown (see Cook's tip below).

5 Return the chicken pieces to the pan, add the diced gammon, onions, green peppers, tomatoes, garlic and thyme and cook, stirring regularly, for 10 minutes, then stir in the prawns.

6 Stir the rice into the pan with one and a half times the rice's volume in cold water. Season with salt, pepper and Tabasco sauce. Bring to the boil and cook over a gentle heat until the rice is tender and the liquid absorbed. Add a little extra boiling water if the rice looks like it is drying out before it is cooked.

7 Mix the spring onions and parsley into the finished dish, reserving a little of the mixture to scatter over the jambalaya as a garnish. Serve hot.

Burgundy Chicken

A dinner-party classic, perfect with a good bottle of red wine.

Serves 4

60ml/4 tbsp plain flour
1.5kg/3lb chicken, cut into 8 joints
15ml/1 tbsp olive oil
65g/2¹/2oz/5 tbsp butter
20 baby onions
75g/3oz piece streaky bacon without rind, diced
about 20 button mushrooms
75cl bottle red Burgundy wine
bouquet garni
3 garlic cloves
5ml/1 tsp soft light brown sugar
salt and black pepper
15ml/1 tbsp chopped fresh parsley and croûtons, to garnish

1 Place 45ml/3 tbsp of the flour and the seasoning in a large plastic bag and shake each chicken joint in it until lightly coated. Heat the oil and 50g/2oz/4 tbsp of the butter in a large flameproof casserole. Add the onions and bacon and sauté for 3–4 minutes, until the onions have browned lightly. Add the mushrooms and fry for 2 minutes. Remove with a slotted spoon into a bowl and reserve.

2 Add the chicken pieces to the hot oil and cook until browned on all sides, about 5–6 minutes. Pour on the Burgundy wine, add the bouquet garni, garlic, soft light brown sugar and seasoning.

3 Bring to the boil, cover and simmer for 1 hour, stirring occasionally.

4 Return the reserved onions, bacon and mushrooms to the casserole, cover and cook for a further 30 minutes.

5 Lift out the cooked chicken, vegetables and bacon with a draining spoon and arrange on a warmed dish. Remove the bouquet garni and boil the liquid rapidly for 2 minutes to reduce slightly. Cream the remaining butter and flour together and whisk in tea-spoonfuls of the mixture until thickened slightly. Pour over the chicken and garnish with parsley and croûtons.

Apricot and Chicken Casserole

*A mild curry and fruity chicken dish
served with almond rice. Makes a
good winter meal.*

INGREDIENTS

Serves 4

15ml/1 tbsp oil

8 chicken thighs, boned and skinned

1 medium onion, finely chopped

5ml/1 tsp medium curry powder

30ml/2 tbsp plain flour

450ml/³/4 pint/1⁷/8 cups chicken
   stock

juice of 1 large orange

8 dried apricots, halved

15ml/1 tbsp sultanas

salt and black pepper

For the almond rice

225g/8oz/2 cups cooked long grain rice

15g/¹/2oz/1 tbsp butter

50g/2oz/¹/2 cup toasted, flaked almonds

1 Preheat the oven to 190°C/
375°F/Gas 5. Heat the oil in a
large frying pan. Cut the chicken
into cubes and brown quickly all
over in the oil. Add the chopped
onion and cook gently until soft
and lightly browned.

2 Transfer the chicken and onion
to a large flameproof casserole
and sprinkle in the curry powder
and cook again for a few minutes.
Add the flour and blend in the
stock and orange juice. Bring to
the boil and season with salt and
freshly ground black pepper.

3 Add the apricots and sultanas,
cover with a lid and cook
gently for an hour, or until tender,
in the preheated oven. Adjust the
seasoning to taste.

4 To make the almond rice,
reheat the pre-cooked rice
with the butter and season to taste.
Stir in the toasted almonds just
before serving.

Chicken in Creamed Horseradish

The piquant flavour of horseradish sauce gives this quick dish a sophisticated taste. Use half the quantity if using fresh horseradish.

INGREDIENTS

Serves 4

30ml/2 tbsp olive oil

4 chicken pieces

25g/1oz/2 tbsp butter

25g/1oz/2 tbsp plain flour

450ml/³/4 pint/1⁷/8 cups chicken stock

30ml/2 tbsp creamed horseradish
   sauce

salt and black pepper

15ml/1 tbsp chopped fresh parsley

mashed potatoes and tender French
   beans, to serve

1 Heat the oil in a large flame-proof casserole and gently brown the chicken joints on both sides over a medium heat. Remove the chicken from the casserole and keep warm.

2 Wipe out the casserole, melt the butter, stir in the flour and blend in the stock gradually. Bring to the boil, stirring all the time.

3 Add the horseradish sauce and season with salt and freshly ground black pepper. Return the chicken to the casserole, cover and simmer for 30–40 minutes or until the chicken is tender.

4 Transfer to a serving dish and sprinkle with fresh parsley. Serve with mashed potatoes and French beans, if desired.

Chicken Paella

There are many variations of this basic recipe. Any seasonal vegetables can be added, together with mussels and other shellfish. Serve straight from the pan.

INGREDIENTS

Serves 4

4 chicken legs (thighs and drumsticks)
60ml/4 tbsp olive oil
1 large onion, finely chopped
1 garlic clove, crushed
5ml/1 tsp ground turmeric
115g/4oz chorizo sausage or smoked ham
225g/8oz/generous 1 cup long grain rice
600ml/1 pint/2^1/2 cups chicken stock
4 tomatoes, skinned, seeded and chopped
1 red pepper, seeded and sliced
115g/4oz/1 cup frozen peas
salt and black pepper

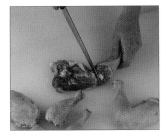

1 Preheat the oven to 180°C/ 350°F/Gas 4. Cut the chicken legs in half.

2 Heat the oil in a 30cm/12in paella pan or large flameproof casserole and brown the chicken pieces on both sides. Add the onion and garlic and stir in the turmeric. Cook for 2 minutes.

3 Slice the sausage or dice the ham and add to the pan, with the rice and stock. Bring to the boil and season to taste, cover and bake for 15 minutes.

4 Remove from the oven and add the chopped tomatoes and sliced red pepper and frozen peas. Return to the oven and cook for a further 10–15 minutes or until the chicken is tender and the rice has absorbed the stock.

Chicken with Peppers

This colourful dish comes from the south of Italy, where sweet peppers are plentiful.

INGREDIENTS

Serves 4

1.5kg/3lb chicken, cut into serving pieces

3 large peppers, red, yellow or green

90ml/6 tbsp olive oil

2 medium red onions, finely sliced

2 cloves garlic, finely chopped

small piece of dried chilli, crumbled
(optional)

100ml/4fl oz/^{1}/2 cup white wine

salt and black pepper

2 tomatoes, fresh or canned, peeled and
chopped

45g/3 tbsp chopped fresh parsley

1 Trim any fat off the chicken, and remove all excess skin. Prepare peppers by cutting them in half, discarding the seeds and the stem. Slice into strips.

2 Heat half the oil in a large heavy saucepan or casserole. Add the onion, and cook over low heat until soft. Remove to a side dish. Add the remaining oil to the pan, raise the heat to moderate, add the chicken and brown on all sides, 6–8 minutes. Return the onions to the pan, and add the garlic and dried chilli, if using.

3 Pour in the wine, and cook until it has reduced by half. Add the peppers and stir well to coat them with the fats. Season. After 3–4 minutes, stir in the tomatoes. Lower the heat, cover the pan, and cook until the peppers are soft, and the chicken is cooked, about 25–30 minutes. Stir occasionally. Stir in the chopped parsley and serve.

Chicken Breasts Cooked in Butter

This simple and very delicious way of cooking chicken brings out all of its delicacy.

INGREDIENTS

Serves 4

4 small chicken breasts, skinned
and boned

flour seasoned with salt and freshly
ground black pepper, for dredging

75g/3oz/6 tbsp butter

1 sprig fresh parsley, to garnish

1 Separate the two fillets of each breast. They come apart very easily; one is large, the other small. Pound the large fillets between two sheets of clear film lightly to flatten them. Dredge the chicken in the seasoned flour, shaking off any excess.

2 Heat the butter in a large heavy frying pan until it bubbles. Place all the chicken fillets in the pan, in one layer if possible. Cook over moderate to high heat for 3–4 minutes until they are golden brown.

3 Turn the chicken over. Reduce the heat to low to moderate, and continue cooking until the fillets are cooked through but still springy to the touch, about 9–12 minutes in all. If the chicken begins to brown too much, cover the pan for the final minutes of cooking. Serve at once garnished with a little parsley.

Chicken in Green Sauce

Slow, gentle cooking makes the chicken succulent and tender.

INGREDIENTS

Serves 4

25g/1oz/2 tbsp butter

15ml/1 tbsp olive oil

4 chicken portions

1 small onion, finely chopped

150ml/^{1}/4 pint/^{2}/3 cup medium dry
    white wine

150ml/^{1}/4 pint/^{2}/3 cup chicken stock

175g/6oz watercress

2 thyme sprigs and 2 tarragon sprigs

150ml/^{1}/4 pint/^{2}/3 cup double cream

salt and black pepper

watercress leaves, to garnish

1 Heat the butter and oil in a heavy shallow pan, then brown the chicken evenly. Transfer the chicken to a plate using a slotted spoon and keep warm in the oven.

2 Add the onion to the cooking juices in the pan and cook until softened but not coloured.

3 Stir in the wine, boil for about 2–3 minutes, then add the stock and bring to the boil. Return the chicken to the pan, cover tightly and cook very gently for about 30 minutes, until the chicken juices run clear. Then transfer the chicken to a warm dish, cover the dish and keep warm.

4 Boil the cooking juices hard until reduced to about 60ml/ 4 tbsp. Remove the leaves from the watercress and herbs, add to the pan with the cream and simmer over a medium heat until the sauce has thickened slightly.

5 Return the cooked chicken to the casserole, season and heat through for a few minutes. Garnish with watercress leaves before serving.

Stoved Chicken

"Stoved" is derived from the French étouffer – to cook in a covered pot – and originates from the Franco/Scottish "Alliance" of the seventeenth century.

Serves 4

1kg/2^{1}/4lb potatoes, cut into 5mm/^{1}/4in slices

2 large onions, thinly sliced

15ml/1 tbsp chopped fresh thyme

25g/1oz/2 tbsp butter

15ml/1 tbsp oil

2 large slices bacon, chopped

4 large chicken joints, halved

bay leaf

600ml/1 pint/2^{1}/2 cups chicken stock

salt and black pepper

1 Preheat the oven to 150°C/ 300°F/Gas 2. Make a thick layer of half the potato slices in the bottom of a large, heavy casserole, then cover with half the onion. Sprinkle with half the thyme, and seasonings.

2 Heat the butter and oil in a large frying pan, then brown the bacon and chicken.

3 Using a slotted spoon, transfer the chicken and bacon to the casserole. Reserve the fat in the pan. Sprinkle the remaining thyme, bay leaf and some seasoning over the chicken, then cover with the remaining onion, followed by a neat layer of overlapping potato slices. Sprinkle with seasoning.

4 Pour the stock into the casserole, brush the potatoes with the reserved fat, then cover tightly and cook in the oven for about 2 hours, until the chicken is tender.

5 Preheat the grill. Uncover the casserole and place under the grill and cook until the slices of potato are beginning to brown and crisp. Serve hot.

Parmesan Chicken Bake

The tomato sauce may be made the day before and left to cool. Serve with crusty bread and salad.

Serves 4

4 chicken breasts, boned and skinned
60ml/4 tbsp plain flour
60ml/4 tbsp olive oil
salt and black pepper

For the tomato sauce

15ml/1 tbsp olive oil
1 onion, finely chopped
1 stick celery, finely chopped
1 red pepper, seeded and diced
1 garlic clove, crushed
400g/14oz can chopped tomatoes with the
  juice
150ml/^{1}/4 pint/^{2}/3 cup chicken stock
15ml/1 tbsp tomato purée
10ml/2 tsp caster sugar
15ml/1 tbsp chopped fresh basil
15ml/1 tbsp chopped fresh parsley

To assemble

225g/8oz mozzarella cheese, sliced
60ml/4 tbsp grated Parmesan cheese
30ml/2 tbsp fresh breadcrumbs

1 To make the tomato sauce, heat 15ml/1 tbsp of the oil in a frying pan and gently cook the onion, celery, pepper and crushed garlic in the oil until tender.

2 Add the tomatoes with their juice, the stock, purée, sugar and herbs. Season to taste and bring to the boil. Simmer for 30 minutes to make a thick sauce, stirring occasionally.

3 Divide the chicken breasts into two natural fillets, place between sheets of clear film and flatten to a thickness of 5mm/^{1}/4in with a rolling pin.

4 Season the flour. Toss the chicken breasts in the flour to coat, shaking to remove the excess.

5 Preheat the oven to 180°C/ 350°F/Gas 4. Heat the remaining oil in a large frying pan and cook the chicken quickly in batches for 3–4 minutes until coloured. Remove and keep warm while frying the rest of the chicken.

6 To assemble, layer the chicken pieces in a large baking dish with the cheeses and thick tomato sauce, finishing with a layer of cheese and breadcrumbs on top. Bake uncovered for 20–30 minutes or until golden brown.

Chicken with Mushrooms

Serve on a dish surrounded with nutty brown rice or tagliatelle verde. White wine or brandy may be used to deglaze the pan in place of sherry.

INGREDIENTS

Serves 4

4 large chicken breasts, boned and skinned

45ml/3 tbsp olive oil

1 onion, thinly sliced

1 garlic clove, crushed

225g/8oz/3 cups button mushrooms, quartered

30ml/2 tbsp sherry

15ml/1 tbsp lemon juice

150ml/¼ pint/⅔ cup single cream

salt and black pepper

3 Add the mushrooms and cook them for a further 5 minutes. Remove and keep warm.

4 Increase the heat. Add the remaining oil and fry the chicken very quickly, in small batches for 3–4 minutes until lightly coloured. Season each batch with a little salt and freshly ground black pepper. Remove and keep warm on a plate while frying the rest of the chicken.

5 Add the sherry and lemon juice to the pan and quickly return the chicken, onions, garlic and mushrooms, stirring to coat.

6 Stir in the cream and bring to the boil. Adjust the seasoning to taste. Serve immediately.

1 Divide the chicken breasts into two natural fillets. Place each between two sheets of clear film and flatten to a thickness of 5mm/¼in with a rolling pin. Cut into 2.5cm/1in diagonal strips.

2 Heat 30ml/2 tbsp of the oil in a large frying pan and cook the onion and crushed garlic slowly until tender.

Chicken with White Wine and Garlic

Add the extra garlic to this dish if you like a stronger flavour.

INGREDIENTS

Serves 4

1.5kg/3¹/₂lb chicken, cut into serving
   pieces
1 onion, sliced
3–6 garlic cloves, to taste, crushed
5ml/1 tsp dried thyme
475ml/16fl oz/2 cups dry white wine
115g/4oz/1 cup green olives (16–18),
   pitted
1 bay leaf
15ml/1 tbsp lemon juice
15–25g/¹/₂–1oz/1–2 tbsp butter
salt and black pepper

1 Heat a deep, heavy frying pan. When hot, add the chicken pieces, skin side down, and cook over medium heat until browned, about 10 minutes. Turn and brown the other side, 5–8 minutes more.

2 Transfer the chicken pieces to a plate and set aside.

3 Drain the excess fat from the frying pan, leaving about 15ml/1 tbsp. Add the sliced onion and 2.5ml/¹/₂ tsp salt and cook until just soft, about 5 minutes. Add the garlic and thyme and cook 1 minute more.

4 Add the wine and stir, scraping up any bits that cling to the pan. Bring to the boil and boil for 1 minute. Stir in the olives.

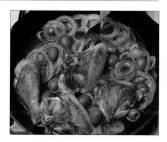

5 Return the chicken pieces to the pan. Add the bay leaf and season lightly with pepper. Lower the heat, cover, and simmer until the chicken is cooked through, about 20–30 minutes.

6 Transfer the chicken pieces to a warmed plate. Stir the lemon juice into the sauce. Whisk in the butter to thicken the sauce slightly. Spoon over the chicken and serve.

Chicken Meat Loaf

Just slice the loaf up and serve it hot or cold.

INGREDIENTS

Serves 4

15ml/1 tbsp olive oil
1 onion, chopped
1 green pepper, seeded and chopped
1 garlic clove, crushed
450g/1lb minced chicken
50g/2oz/1 cup fresh breadcrumbs
1 egg, beaten
50g/2oz/¹/₂ cup pine nuts
12 sun-dried tomatoes in oil, drained and
   chopped
75ml/5 tbsp milk
10ml/2 tsp chopped fresh rosemary, or
   2.5ml/¹/₂ tsp dried rosemary
5ml/1 tsp ground fennel
2.5ml/¹/₂ tsp dried oregano
2.5ml/¹/₂ tsp salt

1 Preheat the oven to 190°C/ 375°F/Gas 5. Heat the oil in a frying pan. Add the onion, green pepper and garlic and cook over low heat, stirring often, until just softened, about 8–10 minutes. Remove from the heat and allow to cool.

2 Place the chicken in a large bowl. Add the onion mixture and the remaining ingredients and mix thoroughly together.

3 Transfer to a 21 x 11 cm/8¹/₂ x 4¹/₂in loaf tin, packing the mixture down firmly. Bake until golden brown, about 1 hour. Serve hot or cold in slices.

French-style Pot-roast Poussins

An incredibly simple dish to make that looks and tastes extra special.

Serves 4

15ml/1 tbsp olive oil

1 onion, sliced

1 large garlic clove, sliced

50g/2oz/scant^1/2 cup diced lightly smoked bacon

2 fresh poussins (just under 450g/1lb each)

30ml/2 tbsp melted butter

2 baby celery hearts, each cut into 4

8 baby carrots

2 small courgettes, cut into chunks

8 small new potatoes

600ml/1 pint/2^1/2 cups chicken stock

150ml/^{1}/4 pint/^{2}/3 cup dry white wine

1 bay leaf

2 fresh thyme sprigs

2 fresh rosemary sprigs

15g/^{1}/2oz/1 tbsp butter, softened

15ml/1 tbsp plain flour

salt and black pepper

fresh herbs, to garnish

1 Preheat the oven to 190°C/375°F/Gas 5. Heat the olive oil in a large flameproof casserole and add the onion, garlic and bacon. Sauté for 5–6 minutes, until the onions have softened.

2 Brush the poussins with a little of the melted butter and season well. Lay on top of the onion mixture and arrange the prepared vegetables around them. Add the chicken stock, wine and herbs.

3 Cover, bake for 20 minutes, then remove the lid and brush the birds with the remaining melted butter. Bake for a further 25–30 minutes until golden.

4 Transfer the poussins to a warmed serving platter and cut each in half with poultry shears or scissors. Remove the vegetables with a draining spoon and arrange them round the birds. Cover with foil and keep warm.

5 Discard the herbs from the pan juices. In a bowl mix together the butter and flour to form a paste. Bring the liquid in the pan to the boil and then whisk in teaspoonfuls of the paste until thickened. Season the sauce and serve with the poussins and vegetables, garnished with fresh herbs.

Coq au Vin

There are many variations to this traditional French dish, but this one is especially delicious. Serve it with warm French bread.

INGREDIENTS

Serves 4

30ml/2 tbsp olive oil

25g/1oz/2 tbsp butter

1.6kg/3^1/2lb chicken, cut into 8 pieces

115g/4oz gammon, cut into 5mm/^{1}/4in strips

115g/4oz button onions, peeled

115g/4oz/1^1/2 cups button mushrooms

2 garlic cloves, crushed

30ml/2 tbsp brandy

250ml/8fl oz/1 cup red wine

300ml/^{1}/2 pint/1^1/4 cups chicken stock

1 bouquet garni

25g/1oz/2 tbsp butter, blended with 30ml/2 tbsp flour

salt and black pepper

chopped parsley, to garnish

1 Preheat the oven to 160°C/ 325°F/Gas 3. Heat the oil and butter in a large flameproof casserole and brown the chicken pieces on all sides.

2 Add the gammon strips, peeled onions, mushrooms and crushed garlic.

3 Pour over the brandy and set it alight. When the flames have subsided add the red wine, stock, bouquet garni and seasoning. Cover and cook slowly for about 1 hour in the preheated oven.

4 Remove the chicken and keep warm. Thicken the sauce with the butter mixture and season to taste. Cook for several minutes and replace the chicken. Sprinkle with chopped parsley and serve.

Chicken in Creamy Orange Sauce

This sauce is deceptively creamy – in fact it is made with low-fat fromage frais, which is virtually fat-free. The brandy adds a richer flavour, but is optional – omit it if you prefer and use orange juice alone.

INGREDIENTS

Serves 4

8 chicken thighs or drumsticks, skinned

45ml/3 tbsp brandy

300ml/^{1}/$_2$ pint/1^1/$_4$ cups orange juice

3 spring onions, chopped

10ml/2 tsp cornflour

90ml/3fl oz/^{1}/$_3$ cup low-fat fromage frais

salt and black pepper

rice or pasta and green salad, to serve

1 Fry the chicken pieces without fat in a non-stick or heavy pan, turning until evenly browned.

2 Stir in the brandy, orange juice and spring onions. Bring to the boil, then cover and simmer for 15 minutes, or until the chicken is tender and the juices run clear, not pink, when pierced.

3 Blend the cornflour with a little water then mix into the fromage frais. Stir this into the sauce and stir over a moderate heat until boiling.

4 Adjust the seasoning and serve with boiled rice or pasta and green salad.

COOK'S TIP

Cornflour helps to stabilize the fromage frais and stop it from curdling.

Tuscan Chicken

This simple peasant casserole has all the flavours of traditional Tuscan ingredients. The wine can be replaced by chicken stock.

Serves 4

8 chicken thighs, skinned

5ml/1 tsp olive oil

1 medium onion, thinly sliced

2 red peppers, seeded and sliced

1 garlic clove, crushed

300ml/^{1}/2 pint/1^1/4 cups passata

150ml/^{1}/4 pint/^{2}/3 cup dry white wine

large sprig fresh oregano, or 5ml/1 tsp
    dried oregano

400g/14oz can cannellini beans, drained

45ml/3 tbsp fresh breadcrumbs

salt and black pepper

1 Fry the chicken in the oil in a non-stick or heavy pan until golden brown. Remove and keep hot. Add the onion and peppers to the pan and gently sauté until softened, but not brown. Stir in the garlic.

2 Add the chicken, passata, wine and oregano. Season well, bring to the boil then cover the pan tightly.

3 Lower the heat and simmer gently, stirring occasionally for 30–35 minutes or until the chicken is tender and the juices run clear, not pink, when pierced with the point of a knife.

4 Stir in the cannellini beans and simmer for a further 5 minutes until heated through. Sprinkle with the breadcrumbs and cook under a hot grill until golden brown.

Koftas in Tomato Sauce

Delicious meatballs in a rich tomato sauce. Serve with pasta and grated Parmesan cheese, if desired.

INGREDIENTS

Serves 4

675g/1^1/2lb chicken
1 onion, grated
1 garlic clove, crushed
15ml/1 tbsp chopped fresh parsley
2.5ml/^{1}/2 tsp ground cumin
2.5ml/^{1}/2 tsp ground coriander
1 egg, beaten
seasoned flour, for rolling
50ml/2fl oz/^{1}/4 cup olive oil
salt and black pepper
chopped fresh parsley, to garnish

For the tomato sauce
15g/^{1}/2oz/1 tbsp butter
15g/^{1}/2oz/2 tbsp plain flour
250ml/8fl oz/1 cup chicken stock
400g/14oz can chopped tomatoes, with
   the juice
5ml/1 tsp caster sugar
1.5ml/^{1}/4 tsp dried mixed herbs

1 Preheat the oven to 180°C/ 350°F/Gas 4. Remove any skin and bone from the chicken and mince or chop finely.

2 Put into a bowl together with the onion, garlic, parsley, spices, seasoning and beaten egg.

3 Mix together thoroughly and shape into 24 x 4cm/1^1/2in balls. Roll lightly in seasoned flour.

4 Heat the oil in a frying pan and brown the balls in small batches (this keeps the oil temperature hot and prevents the flour becoming soggy). Remove and drain on kitchen paper. There is no need to cook the balls any further at this stage as they will cook in the tomato sauce.

5 To make the tomato sauce, melt the butter in a large saucepan. Add the flour, and then blend in the stock and tomatoes along with their juice. Add the caster sugar and mixed herbs. Bring to the boil, cover and simmer for 10–15 minutes.

6 Place the browned chicken balls into a shallow ovenproof dish and pour over the tomato sauce, cover with foil and bake in the preheated oven for 30–40 minutes. Adjust the seasoning to taste and sprinkle with parsley.

Spanish Chicken

A colourful one pot dish, ideal for entertaining and delicious served with a crisp green salad.

INGREDIENTS

Serves 8

30ml/2 tbsp plain flour
10ml/2 tsp ground paprika
2.5ml/^{1}/$_2$ tsp salt
16 chicken drumsticks
50ml/2fl oz/^{1}/$_4$ cup olive oil
1.2 litres/2 pints/5 cups chicken stock
1 onion, finely chopped
2 garlic cloves, crushed
450g/1lb/2^2/$_3$ cups long grain rice
2 bay leaves
225g/8oz/1^1/$_3$ cups diced cooked ham
115g/4oz/1 cup pimento-stuffed green olives
1 green pepper, seeded and diced
2 x 400g/14oz cans chopped tomatoes, with the juice
60ml/4 tbsp chopped fresh parsley

1 Preheat the oven to 180°C/ 350°F/Gas 4. Shake together the flour, paprika and salt in a plastic bag, add the drumsticks and toss to coat.

2 Heat the oil in a large flame-proof casserole and, working in batches, brown the chicken drumsticks slowly on all sides. Remove and keep warm.

3 Meanwhile, bring the stock to the boil and add the onion, crushed garlic, rice and bay leaves. Cook for 10 minutes. Draw aside and add the ham, olives, peppers, and canned tomatoes with their juice. Transfer to a shallow oven-proof dish.

4 Arrange the chicken on top, cover and bake for 30–40 minutes or until tender. Add a little more stock if necessary to prevent from drying out. Remove the bay leaves and sprinkle over the chopped parsley to garnish.

Chicken with Lemon and Herbs

The herbs can be changed according to what is available; for example, parsley or thyme could be used instead of tarragon and fennel.

INGREDIENTS

Serves 2

50g/2oz/4 tbsp butter
2 spring onions, white part only, finely
  chopped
15ml/1 tbsp chopped fresh tarragon
15ml/1 tbsp chopped fresh fennel
juice of 1 lemon
4 chicken thighs
salt and black pepper
lemon slices and herb sprigs, to garnish

1 Preheat the grill to moderate. In a small saucepan, melt the butter, then add the spring onions, herbs, lemon juice and seasoning.

2 Brush the chicken generously with the herb mixture, then grill for 10–12 minutes, basting frequently with the herb mixture.

3 Turn over, baste again, then cook for a further 10 minutes or until the juices run clear.

4 Serve garnished with lemon and herbs and with any remaining herb mixture.

Chicken with Red Cabbage

Chestnuts and red cabbage make a colourful winter dish.

INGREDIENTS

Serves 4

50g/2oz/4 tbsp butter
4 large chicken portions, halved
1 onion, chopped
500g/1¼lb red cabbage, finely shredded
4 juniper berries, crushed
12 cooked peeled chestnuts
120ml/4fl oz/½ cup full-bodied red wine
salt and black pepper

1 Heat the butter in a heavy flameproof casserole and lightly brown the chicken pieces. Transfer to a plate.

2 Add the onion to the casserole and fry gently until soft and light golden brown. Stir the cabbage and juniper berries into the casserole, season and cook over a moderate heat for 6–7 minutes, stirring once or twice.

3 Stir the chestnuts into the casserole, then tuck the chicken pieces under the cabbage so they are on the bottom of the casserole. Pour in the red wine.

4 Cover and cook gently for about 40 minutes until the chicken juices run clear and the cabbage is very tender. Check the seasoning and serve.

Chicken with Blackberries and Lemon

This delicious stew combines some wonderful flavours. The red wine and blackberries give it a dramatic appearance.

INGREDIENTS

Serves 4

4 part-boned chicken breasts
25g/1oz/2 tbsp butter
15ml/1 tbsp sunflower oil
25g/1oz/4 tbsp flour
150ml/^{1}/4 pint/^{2}/3 cup red wine
150ml/^{1}/4 pint/^{2}/3 cup chicken stock
grated rind of ^{1}/2 orange plus 15ml/1 tbsp juice
3 sprigs lemon balm, finely chopped, plus 1 sprig to garnish
150ml/^{1}/4 pint/^{2}/3 cup double cream
1 egg yolk
115g/4oz/1 cup fresh blackberries, plus 50g/2oz/^{1}/2 cup to garnish
salt and black pepper

1 Preheat the oven to 180°C/ 350°F/Gas 4. Remove any skin from the chicken, and season the meat. Heat the butter and oil in a frying pan, fry the chicken to seal it, then transfer to a casserole dish. Stir the flour into the pan, then add the wine and stock and bring to the boil. Add the orange rind and juice, and the chopped lemon balm. Pour over the chicken.

2 Cover the casserole and cook in the oven for about 40 minutes.

3 Blend the cream with the egg yolk, add some of the liquid from the casserole and stir back into the dish with the blackberries (reserving those for the garnish). Cover and cook for another 10–15 minutes. Serve garnished with the rest of the blackberries and the sprig of lemon balm.

Chicken with Cajun Sauce

*Sizzling fried chicken served in a
tasty tomato sauce.*

Serves 4

1.6kg/3^1/2lb chicken, cut into 8 pieces
90g/3^1/2oz/^{3}/4 cup plain flour
250ml/8fl oz/1 cup buttermilk or milk
vegetable oil, for frying
salt and black pepper
chopped spring onions, to garnish

For the sauce

115g/4oz/^{2}/3 cup lard or vegetable oil
65g/2^1/2oz/9 tbsp flour
2 onions, chopped
2–3 celery sticks, chopped
1 large green pepper, seeded and chopped
2 garlic cloves, finely chopped
250ml/8fl oz/1 cup passata
450ml/^{3}/4 pint/1^7/8 cups red wine or
    chicken stock
225g/8oz/1^3/4 cups tomatoes, skinned and
    chopped
2 bay leaves
15ml/1 tbsp soft brown sugar
5ml/1 tsp grated orange rind
2.5ml/^{1}/2 tsp cayenne pepper

1 To make the sauce, heat the
lard or oil in a large, heavy pan
and stir in the flour. Cook over
moderately low heat, stirring constantly, for 15–20 minutes or until
the mixture has darkened to the
colour of hazelnut shells.

2 Add the chopped onions,
celery, green pepper and garlic
and cook, stirring, until the
vegetables are softened.

3 Stir in the remaining sauce
ingredients with salt and
pepper to taste. Bring to the boil,
then simmer for 1 hour or until
the sauce is rich and thick. Stir
from time to time.

4 Meanwhile, prepare the
chicken. Put the flour in a
plastic bag and season with salt
and pepper. Dip each piece of
chicken in buttermilk, then dredge
in the flour to coat lightly all over.
Shake off excess flour. Set the
chicken aside for 20 minutes to let
the coating set before frying.

5 Heat the vegetable oil
2.5cm/1in deep in a large
frying pan until it is very hot and
starting to sizzle. Fry the chicken
pieces, turning them once, for
about 30 minutes or until deep
golden brown all over and cooked
through.

6 Drain the chicken pieces on
paper towels. Add them to the
sauce and sprinkle with chopped
spring onions.

Pot-roast Chicken with Sausage Stuffing

These casseroled chickens will be tender and succulent.

INGREDIENTS

Serves 6

2 x 1.12kg/2¹/₂lb chickens
30ml/2 tbsp vegetable oil
350ml/12fl oz/1¹/₂ cups chicken stock or
   half wine and half stock
1 bay leaf

For the stuffing
450g/1lb sausagemeat
1 small onion, chopped
1–2 garlic cloves, finely chopped
5ml/1 tsp hot paprika
2.5ml/¹/₂ tsp dried chilli (optional)
2.5ml/¹/₂ tsp dried thyme
1.5ml/¹/₄ tsp ground allspice
40g/1¹/₂oz/1 cup coarse fresh breadcrumbs
1 egg, beaten to mix
salt and black pepper

1 Preheat the oven to 180°C/
350°F/Gas 4.

2 For the stuffing, put the sausagemeat, onion and garlic in a frying pan and fry over moderate heat until the sausagemeat is lightly browned and crumbly, stirring and turning so it cooks evenly. Remove from the heat and mix in the remaining stuffing ingredients with salt and pepper to taste.

3 Divide the stuffing between the chickens, packing it into the body cavities (or, if preferred, stuff the neck end and bake the leftover stuffing in a separate dish). Truss the birds.

4 Heat the oil in a flameproof casserole just big enough to hold the chickens. Brown the birds all over.

5 Add the stock and bay leaf and season. Cover and bring to the boil, then transfer to the oven. Pot-roast for 1¹/₄ hours or until the birds are cooked (the juices will run clear).

6 Untruss the chickens and spoon the stuffing on to a serving platter. Arrange the birds and serve with the strained cooking liquid.

VARIATION

For Pot-roast Guinea Fowl, use 2 guinea fowl instead of chickens.

Poussins Waldorf

Sunday roast and stuffing, with a difference.

INGREDIENTS

Serves 6

6 poussins, each weighing about
   500g/1^1/4lb
salt and black pepper
40–50g/1^1/2–2oz/3–4 tbsp butter, melted

For the stuffing
25g/1oz/2 tbsp butter
1 onion, finely chopped
300g/11oz/2^1/4 cups cooked rice
2 celery sticks, finely chopped
2 red apples, cored and finely diced
50g/2oz/^{1}/3 cup walnuts, chopped
75ml/5 tbsp cream sherry or apple juice
30ml/2 tbsp lemon juice

1 Preheat the oven to 180°C/
350°F/Gas 4. To make the
stuffing, melt the butter in a small
frying pan and fry the onion,
stirring occasionally, until soft. Tip
the onion and butter into a bowl
and add the remaining stuffing
ingredients. Season with salt and
pepper and mix well.

2 Divide the stuffing among the
poussins, stuffing the body
cavities. Truss the birds and
arrange in a roasting tin. Sprinkle
with salt and pepper and drizzle
over the melted butter.

3 Roast for about 1^1/4–1^1/2 hours.
Untruss before serving.

CARVING POULTRY

Carving a bird neatly for serving makes the present-
ation attractive. You will need a sharp long-bladed
knife, or an electric knife, plus a long 2-pronged fork
and a carving board with a well to catch the juices.

Cut away any trussing string. For a stuffed bird,
spoon the stuffing from the cavity into a serving
dish. For easier carving, remove the wishbone.

Insert the fork into one breast to hold the bird
steady. Cut through the skin to the ball and socket
joint on that side of the body, then slice through it to
sever the leg from the body. Repeat on the other side.

1 Slice through the ball and socket joint in each leg
to sever the thigh and drumstick. If carving
turkey, slice the meat off the thigh and drumstick,
parallel to the bone, turning to get even slices; leave
chicken thighs and drumsticks whole.

2 To carve the breast of a turkey or chicken, cut
5mm/^{1}/4in thick slices at an angle, slicing down
on both sides of the breastbone. For smaller birds,
remove the meat on each side of the breastbone in a
single piece, then slice across.

Chicken Brunswick Stew

This is chicken stew with a spicy bite, warming and filling.

Serves 6

1.75kg/4lb chicken, cut in serving pieces
paprika
30ml/2 tbsp olive oil
30ml/2 tbsp butter
450g/1lb/2 cups chopped onions
225g/^{1}/2lb/1 cup chopped green or yellow
    peppers
475ml/16 fl oz/2 cups chopped peeled
    fresh or canned plum tomatoes
250ml/8fl oz/1 cup white wine
475ml/16fl oz/2 cups chicken stock or
    water
15g/^{1}/2oz/^{1}/4 cup chopped fresh parsley
2.5ml/^{1}/2 tsp hot pepper sauce
15ml/1 tbsp Worcestershire sauce
350g/12oz/2 cups sweetcorn (fresh, frozen
    or canned)
185g/6^1/2oz/1 cup butter beans (fresh or
    frozen)
45ml/3 tbsp flour
salt and black pepper
rolls, rice, or potatoes, for serving
    (optional)

1 Pat the chicken pieces dry, then sprinkle them lightly with salt and paprika.

2 In a large heavy saucepan, heat the olive oil with the butter over medium-high heat. Heat until the mixture is sizzling and just starting to change colour.

3 Add the chicken pieces and fry until golden brown on all sides. Remove the chicken pieces with tongs and set aside.

4 Reduce the heat to low and add the chopped onions and peppers to the pan. Cook until softened, 8–10 minutes.

5 Raise the heat. Add the tomatoes and their juice, the wine, stock or water, parsley, and hot pepper and Worcestershire sauces. Stir and bring to the boil.

6 Return the fried chicken pieces to the pan, pushing it down in the sauce. Cover, reduce the heat, and simmer 30 minutes, stirring occasionally.

7 Add the sweetcorn and butter beans and mix well. Partly cover and cook 30 minutes more.

8 Tilt the pan and skim off as much of the surface fat as possible. In a small bowl, mix the flour with a little water to make a paste.

9 Gradually stir in about 175ml/6fl oz/^{3}/4 cup of the hot sauce from the pan. Stir the flour mixture into the stew, and mix well to distribute it evenly and thicken. Cook 5–8 minutes more, stirring from time to time.

10 Check the seasoning. Serve the stew in shallow soup plates or large bowls.

Chicken with Sage, Prunes and Brandy

This stir-fry has a very rich sauce based on a good brandy – use the best you can afford.

INGREDIENTS

Serves 4

115g/4oz prunes

1.5kg/3–3^1/2lb boneless chicken breast

300ml/^{1}/2 pint/1^1/4 cups cognac or brandy

15ml/1 tbsp fresh sage, chopped

150g/5oz smoked bacon, in one piece

50g/2oz/4 tbsp butter

24 baby onions, peeled and quartered

salt and black pepper

fresh sage sprigs, to garnish

1 Stone the prunes and cut them into slivers. Remove the skin from the chicken and cut the breast into thin pieces.

2 Mix together the prunes, chicken, cognac and chopped sage in a non-metallic dish. Cover and leave to marinate overnight.

3 Next day, strain the chicken and prunes, reserving the cognac marinade mixture, and pat dry on kitchen towels.

4 Cut the smoked bacon into dice and set aside.

5 Heat the wok and add half the butter. When melted, add the onions and stir-fry for 4 minutes until crisp and golden. Set aside.

6 Add the bacon to the wok and stir-fry for 1 minute until it begins to release some fat. Add the remaining butter and stir-fry the chicken and prunes for 3–4 minutes until crisp and golden. Push the chicken mixture to one side in the wok, add the cognac and simmer until thickened. Stir the chicken into the sauce, season well with salt and pepper, and serve garnished with sage.

Pasta Sauce with Chicken and Tomato

Perfect for a speedy supper – serve this with a mixed bean salad.

Serves 4

15ml/1 tbsp olive oil

1 onion, chopped

1 carrot, chopped

50g/2oz/1 cup sun-dried tomatoes in olive oil, drained weight

1 garlic clove, chopped

400g/14oz can chopped tomatoes, drained

15ml/1 tbsp tomato purée

150ml/$^1/4$ pint/$^2/3$ cup chicken stock

350g/12oz/3 cups pasta spirals (fusilli)

225g/8oz chicken, diagonally sliced

salt and black pepper

sprigs fresh mint, to garnish

1 Heat the oil in a large frying pan and fry the chopped onion and carrot for 5 minutes, stirring from time to time.

2 Chop the sun-dried tomatoes and set aside.

3 Stir the garlic, canned tomatoes, tomato purée and stock into the onions and carrots and bring to the boil. Simmer for 10 minutes, stirring occasionally.

4 Cook the pasta in plenty of water, according to the instructions on the packet.

5 Pour the sauce into a food processor or blender and process until smooth.

COOK'S TIP
~

Sun-dried tomatoes are sold soaked in vegetable or olive oil in jars. The olive oil-soaked tomatoes have a superior flavour. For extra flavour, fry the onion and carrot in 15ml/1 tbsp of the oil from the tomatoes.

6 Return the sauce to the pan and stir in the sun-dried tomatoes and chicken. Bring back to the boil, then simmer for 10 minutes until the chicken is cooked. Adjust the seasoning.

7 Drain the pasta thoroughly and toss it in the sauce. Serve immediately, garnished with sprigs of fresh mint.

Chicken with Sloe Gin and Juniper

Juniper is used in the manufacture of gin, and the reinforcement of the flavour by using both sloe gin and juniper is delicious. Sloe gin is easy to make, but can also be bought ready-made.

INGREDIENTS

Serves 8

25g/1oz/2 tbsp butter
30ml/2 tbsp sunflower oil
8 chicken breast fillets
350g/12oz carrots, cooked
1 clove garlic, crushed
15ml/1 tbsp finely chopped parsley
50ml/2fl oz/^{1}/4 cup chicken stock
50ml/2fl oz/^{1}/4 cup red wine
50ml/2fl oz/^{1}/4 cup sloe gin
5ml/1 tsp crushed juniper berries
salt and black pepper
chopped fresh basil, to garnish

1 Melt the butter with the oil in a frying pan, and fry the chicken until browned on all sides.

2 In a food processor or blender, combine all the remaining ingredients except the basil, and blend to a smooth purée. If the mixture seems too thick add a little more red wine or water.

3 Put the chicken breast in a clean pan, pour the sauce over the top and cook over a medium heat until the chicken is cooked through – about 15 minutes. Adjust the seasoning and serve garnished with chopped basil.

Chicken with Figs and Mint

Refreshing mint and orange flavours go well with chicken.

INGREDIENTS

Serves 4

500g/1^1/4lb/3^1/3 cups dried figs

^{1}/2 bottle sweet, fruity white wine

4 boneless chicken breasts, about 175–225g/6–8oz each

15ml/1 tbsp butter

30ml/2 tbsp dark orange marmalade

10 mint leaves, finely chopped, plus a few more to garnish

juice of ^{1}/2 lemon

salt and black pepper

1 Place the figs in a pan with the wine and bring to the boil, then simmer very gently for about 1 hour. Leave to cool and refrigerate overnight.

2 Fry the chicken breasts in the butter until they are cooked. Remove and keep warm. Drain any fat from the pan and pour in the juice from the figs. Boil and reduce to about 150ml/^{1}/4 pint/^{2}/3 cup.

3 Add the marmalade, chopped mint leaves and lemon juice, and simmer for a few minutes. Season to taste. When the sauce is thick and shiny, pour it over the meat, garnish with the figs and mint leaves and serve.

Chicken Sauce Piquante

Sauce Piquante goes with everything that runs, flies or swims in Louisiana – you will even find Alligator Sauce Piquante on menus. It is based on the brown Cajun roux and chilli peppers give it heat: vary the heat by the number you use.

Serves 4

4 chicken legs or 2 legs and 2 breasts
75ml/3fl oz/^{1}/3 cup cooking oil
50g/2oz/^{1}/2 cup plain flour
1 medium onion, chopped
2 celery sticks, sliced
1 green pepper, seeded and diced
2 garlic cloves, crushed
1 bay leaf
2.5ml/^{1}/2 tsp dried thyme
2.5ml/^{1}/2 tsp dried oregano
1–2 red chilli peppers, seeded and finely
    chopped
400g/14oz can tomatoes, chopped, with
    the juice
300ml/^{1}/2 pint/1^1/4 cups chicken stock
salt and black pepper
watercress to garnish
boiled potatoes to serve

1 Halve the chicken legs through the joint, or the breasts across the middle, to give 8 pieces.

2 In a heavy frying pan, fry the chicken pieces in the oil until brown on all sides, setting them aside as they are done.

3 Strain the oil from the pan into a heavy flameproof casserole. Heat it and stir in the flour. Stir constantly over a low heat until the roux is the colour of peanut butter.

4 Immediately the roux reaches the right stage, tip in the onion, celery and pepper and stir over the heat for 2–3 minutes.

5 Add the garlic, bay leaf, thyme, oregano and chilli pepper(s). Stir for 1 minute, then turn down the heat and stir in the tomatoes with their juice.

6 Return the casserole to the heat and gradually stir in the stock. Add the chicken pieces, cover and leave to simmer for 45 minutes, until the chicken is tender.

7 If there is too much sauce or if it looks too runny, remove the lid for the last 10–15 minutes of the cooking time and turn up the heat a little.

8 Check the seasoning and serve garnished with watercress and accompanied by boiled potatoes.

COOK'S TIP

If you prefer to err on the side of caution with chilli heat, use just 1 chilli pepper and hot up the seasoning at the end with a dash or two of Tabasco sauce.
The oil in chilli peppers clings to your skin and could hurt if you then rub your eyes. Scrape out the seeds under running cold water and wash your hands after handling chillies.

Stuffed Chicken Wings

These tasty stuffed wings can be served hot or cold at a buffet. They can be prepared and frozen in advance.

Makes 12

12 large chicken wings

For the filling

5ml/1 tsp cornflour
1.5ml/^{1}/4 tsp salt
2.5ml/^{1}/2 tsp fresh thyme
pinch of black pepper

For the coating

225g/8oz/3 cups dried breadcrumbs
30ml/2 tbsp sesame seeds
2 eggs, beaten
oil, for deep-frying

1 Remove the wing tips and discard or use them for making stock. Skin the second joint sections, removing the two small bones and reserve the meat for the filling.

2 Mince the reserved meat and mix with the filling ingredients.

3 Holding the large end of the bone on the third section of the wing and using a sharp knife, cut the skin and flesh away from the bone, scraping down and pulling the meat over the small end forming a pocket. Repeat this process with the remaining wing sections.

4 Fill the tiny pockets with the filling. Mix the dried breadcrumbs and the sesame seeds together. Place the breadcrumb mixture and the beaten egg in separate dishes.

5 Brush the meat with beaten egg and roll in breadcrumbs to cover. Chill and repeat to give a second layer, forming a thick coating. Chill until ready to fry.

6 Preheat the oven to 180°C/350°F/Gas 4. Heat 5cm/2in of oil in a heavy-based pan until hot but not smoking or the breadcrumbs will burn. Gently fry two or three wings at a time until golden brown, remove and drain on kitchen paper. Complete the cooking in the preheated oven for 15–20 minutes or until tender.

Penne with Chicken and Ham Sauce

A meal in itself, this colourful pasta sauce is perfect for lunch or dinner.

Serves 4

350g/12oz/3 cups penne pasta
25g/1oz/2 tbsp butter
1 onion, chopped
1 garlic clove, chopped
1 bay leaf
475ml/16 fl oz/2 cups dry white wine
150ml/^{1}/4 pint/^{2}/3 cup crème fraîche
225g/8oz/1^1/2 cups cooked chicken, skinned, boned and diced
115g/4oz/^{2}/3 cup cooked lean ham, diced
115g/4oz/1 cup Gouda cheese, grated
15ml/1 tbsp chopped fresh mint
salt and black pepper
finely shredded fresh mint, to garnish

1 Cook the pasta in plenty of water, according to the instructions on the packet.

2 Heat the butter in a large frying pan and fry the onion for 10 minutes until softened.

COOK'S TIP

Crème fraîche is a richer, full-fat French cream with a slightly acidic taste. If you can't find any, substitute soured cream.

3 Add the garlic, bay leaf and wine and bring to the boil. Boil rapidly until reduced by half. Remove the bay leaf, then stir in the crème fraîche and bring back to the boil.

4 Add the chicken, ham and cheese and simmer for about 5 minutes, stirring occasionally until heated through.

5 Add the mint and seasoning. Drain the pasta and turn it into a large serving bowl. Toss with the sauce immediately and garnish with shredded mint.

Tagliatelle with Chicken and Herb Sauce

*This wine-flavoured sauce is best
served with green salad.*

INGREDIENTS

Serves 4

30ml/2 tbsp olive oil
1 red onion, cut into wedges
350g/12oz tagliatelle
1 garlic clove, chopped
350g/12oz/2¹/₂ cups chicken, diced
300ml/¹/₂ pint/1¹/₄ cups dry vermouth
45ml/3 tbsp chopped fresh mixed herbs
150ml/¹/₄ pint/²/₃ cup fromage frais
salt and black pepper
shredded fresh mint, to garnish

1 Heat the oil in a large frying
pan and fry the onion for
10 minutes until softened and the
layers separate.

2 Cook the pasta in plenty of
water, according to the
instructions on the packet.

COOK'S TIP

If you don't want to use
vermouth, use dry white wine
instead. Orvieto and frascati are
two Italian wines that are ideal to
use in this sauce.

3 Add the garlic and chicken to
the pan and fry for 10 minutes,
stirring occasionally until the
chicken is browned all over and
cooked through.

4 Pour in the vermouth, bring to
the boil and boil rapidly until
reduced by about half.

5 Stir in the herbs, fromage frais
and seasoning and heat
through gently, but do not boil.

6 Drain the pasta thoroughly and
toss it with the sauce to coat.
Serve immediately, garnished with
shredded fresh mint.

Risotto

An Italian dish made with short grain arborio rice which gives a creamy consistency to this easy one-pan recipe.

INGREDIENTS

Serves 4

15ml/1 tbsp oil

175g/6oz/1 cup Arborio rice

1 onion, chopped

225g/8oz/2 cups minced chicken

600ml/1 pint/2^{1}/2 cups chicken stock

1 red pepper, seeded and chopped

1 yellow pepper, seeded and chopped

75g/3oz/^{3}/4 cup frozen green beans

115g/4oz/1^{1}/2 cups chestnut mushrooms, sliced

15ml/1 tbsp chopped fresh parsley

salt and black pepper

fresh parsley, to garnish

3 Pour in the stock and bring to the boil.

4 Stir in the peppers and reduce the heat. Cook for 10 minutes.

5 Add the green beans and mushrooms and cook for a further 10 minutes.

6 Stir in the fresh parsley and season well to taste. Cook for 10 minutes or until the liquid has been absorbed. Serve garnished with fresh parsley.

1 Heat the oil in a large frying pan. Add the rice and cook for 2 minutes until transparent.

2 Add the onion and minced chicken. Cook for 5 minutes, stirring occasionally.

SALADS
& BARBECUES

Chicken Pittas with Red Coleslaw

Pittas are convenient for simple snacks and packed lunches and it's easy to pack them with lots of fresh, healthy ingredients.

INGREDIENTS

Serves 4

$1/4$ red cabbage, finely shredded
1 small red onion, finely sliced
2 radishes, thinly sliced
1 red apple, peeled, cored and
    grated
15ml/1 tbsp lemon juice
45ml/3 tbsp fromage frais
1 cooked chicken breast without
    skin, about 175g/6oz
4 large pittas or 8 small pittas
salt and black pepper
chopped fresh parsley, to garnish

1 Remove the tough central spine from the cabbage leaves, then finely shred the leaves using a large sharp knife. Place the shredded cabbage in a bowl and stir in the onion, radishes, apple and lemon juice.

2 Stir the fromage frais into the shredded cabbage mixture and season well with salt and pepper. Thinly slice the cooked chicken breast and stir into the shredded cabbage mixture until well coated in fromage frais.

3 Sprinkle the pittas with a little water, then warm them under a hot grill, then split them along one edge using a round-bladed knife. Share the filling equally among the pittas, then garnish with chopped fresh parsley.

COOK'S TIP

If the filled pittas need to be made more than an hour in advance, line the pitta breads with crisp lettuce leaves before adding the filling.

Caribbean Chicken Kebabs

These kebabs have a rich, sunshine Caribbean flavour and the marinade keeps them moist without the need for oil. Serve with a colourful salad and rice.

INGREDIENTS

Serves 4

500g/1¼lb chicken breasts, boned and skinned

finely grated rind of 1 lime

30ml/2 tbsp lime juice

15ml/1 tbsp rum or sherry

15ml/1 tbsp light muscovado sugar

5ml/1 tsp ground cinnamon

2 mangoes, peeled and cubed

rice and salad, to serve

1 Cut the chicken breasts into bite-size chunks and place in a bowl with the grated lime rind and juice, rum or sherry, sugar and cinnamon. Toss well, cover and leave to marinate for 1 hour.

COOK'S TIP
~

The rum or sherry adds a lovely rich flavour, but it is optional so can be omitted if you prefer to make the dish more economical.

2 Save the juices and thread the chicken on to four wooden skewers, alternating with the mango cubes.

3 Cook the skewers under a hot grill or barbecue for 8–10 minutes, turning occasionally and basting with the reserved juices, until the chicken is tender and golden brown. Serve at once with rice and salad.

Grilled Chicken

The flavour of the dish, known in Indonesia as Ayam Bakur, *will be more intense if the chicken is marinated overnight. It is an ideal recipe for a party, because the final grilling, barbecuing or baking can be done at the last minute.*

INGREDIENTS

Serves 4

1.5kg/3–3^{1}/2lb chicken
4 garlic cloves, crushed
2 lemon grass stems, lower 2 inch sliced
1 teaspoon ground turmeric
475ml/16fl oz/2 cups water
3–4 bay leaves
45ml/3 tbsp each dark and light soy sauce
50g/2oz/^{1}/4 cup butter or margarine
salt
boiled rice, to serve

1 Cut the chicken into 4 or 8 portions. Slash the fleshy part of each portion twice and set aside.

2 Grind the garlic, sliced lemon grass, turmeric and salt together into a paste in a food processor or with a mortar and pestle. Rub the paste into the chicken pieces and leave for at least 30 minutes. Wear rubber gloves for this, as the turmeric will stain heavily; or wash your hands immediately after mixing, if you prefer.

3 Transfer the chicken to a wok and pour in the water. Add the bay leaves and bring to a boil. Cover and cook gently for 30 minutes, adding a little more water if necessary and stirring from time to time.

4 Just before serving, add the two soy sauces to the pan together with the butter or margarine.

5 Cook until the chicken is well-coated and the sauce has almost been absorbed. Transfer the chicken to a preheated grill or barbecue, or an oven preheated to 200°C/400°F/Gas 6, to complete the cooking. Cook for a further 10–15 minutes, turning the pieces often so they become golden brown all over. Take care not to let them burn. Baste with remaining sauce during cooking. Serve with boiled rice.

Dijon Chicken Salad

An attractive dish to serve for lunch with herb and garlic bread.

Serves 4

4 chicken breasts, boned and skinned
mixed salad leaves, e.g. frisée and oakleaf
lettuce or radicchio, to serve

For the marinade
30ml/2 tbsp Dijon mustard
3 garlic cloves, crushed
15ml/1 tbsp grated onion
60ml/4 tbsp white wine

For the mustard dressing
30ml/2 tbsp tarragon wine vinegar
5ml/1 tsp Dijon mustard
5ml/1 tsp clear honey
90ml/6 tbsp olive oil
salt and black pepper

1 Mix all the marinade ingredients together in a shallow glass or earthenware dish that is large enough to hold the chicken in a single layer.

2 Turn the chicken over in the marinade to coat completely, cover with clear film and then chill in the fridge overnight.

3 Preheat the oven to 190°C/375°F/Gas 5. Transfer the chicken and the marinade into an ovenproof dish, cover with foil and bake for about 35 minutes or until tender. Leave to cool.

4 Put all the mustard dressing ingredients into a screw-topped jar, shake vigorously to emulsify, and adjust the seasoning. (This can be made several days in advance and stored in the fridge.)

5 Slice the chicken thinly, fan out the slices and arrange on a serving dish with the salad leaves.

6 Spoon over some of the mustard dressing and serve.

Lemon Chicken with Guacamole Sauce

The avocado sauce makes an unusual accompaniment to the grilled chicken.

Serves 4

juice of 2 lemons

45ml/3 tbsp olive oil

2 garlic cloves, crushed

4 chicken breast halves, about 200g/7oz each

2 beefsteak tomatoes, cored and cut in half

salt and black pepper

chopped fresh coriander, for garnishing

For the sauce

1 ripe avocado

50ml/2 fl oz/¹/₄ cup sour cream

45ml/3 tbsp fresh lemon juice

25ml/¹/₂ tsp salt

50ml/2 fl oz/¹/₄ cup water

1 Combine the lemon juice, oil, garlic, ¹/₂ tsp salt, and a little pepper in a bowl. Stir to mix.

2 Arrange the chicken breasts, in one layer, in a shallow glass or ceramic dish. Pour over the lemon mixture and turn to coat evenly. Cover and let stand at least 1 hour at room temperature, or refrigerate overnight.

3 For the sauce, cut the avocado in half, remove the pit, and scrape the flesh into a food processor or blender.

4 Add the sour cream, lemon juice, and salt and process until smooth. Add the water and process just to blend. If necessary, add more water to thin the sauce. Transfer to a bowl, taste and adjust the seasoning, if necessary. Set aside.

5 Preheat the grill. Heat a ridged frying pan. Remove the chicken from the marinade and pat dry.

6 When the grill pan is hot, add the chicken breasts and cook, turning often, until they are cooked through, about 10 minutes.

7 Meanwhile, arrange the tomato halves, cut-sides up, on a baking sheet and season lightly with salt and pepper. Grill until hot and bubbling, about 5 minutes.

8 To serve, place a chicken breast, tomato half, and a dollop of avocado sauce on each plate. Sprinkle with coriander and serve.

VARIATION

To barbecue the chicken, light the barbecue, and when the coals are glowing red and covered with grey ash, spread them in a single layer. Set an oiled grill rack about 12cm/ 5in above the coals and cook the chicken breasts until lightly charred and cooked through, about 15–20 minutes. Allow extra olive oil for basting.

Chicken Liver Kebabs

These may be barbecued outdoors and served with salads and baked potatoes or grilled indoors and served with rice and broccoli.

INGREDIENTS

Serves 4

115g/4oz rindless streaky bacon rashers
350g/12oz chicken livers
12 large ready-to-eat stoned prunes
12 cherry tomatoes
8 button mushrooms
30ml/2 tbsp olive oil

1 Cut each rasher of bacon into two pieces, wrap a piece around each chicken liver and secure in position with wooden cocktail sticks.

2 Wrap the stoned prunes around the cherry tomatoes.

3 Thread the bacon-wrapped livers on to metal skewers with the tomatoes and prunes. Brush with oil. Cover the tomatoes and prunes with a strip of foil to protect them while grilling or barbecuing. Cook for 5 minutes on each side.

4 Remove the cocktail sticks and serve the kebabs immediately.

Citrus Kebabs

Serve on a bed of lettuce leaves and garnish with fresh mint and orange and lemon slices.

Serves 4

4 chicken breasts, skinned and boned
sprigs fresh mint, to garnish
orange, lemon or lime slices, to garnish
  (optional)

For the marinade
finely grated rind and juice of $^1/_2$ orange
finely grated rind and juice of $^1/_2$ small
  lemon or lime
30ml/2 tbsp olive oil
30ml/2 tbsp clear honey
30ml/2 tbsp chopped fresh mint
1.5ml/$^1/_4$ tsp ground cumin
salt and black pepper

1 Cut the chicken into cubes of approximately 2.5cm/1in.

2 Mix the marinade ingredients together in a glass or ceramic bowl, add the chicken cubes and leave them to marinate for at least 2 hours.

3 Thread the chicken pieces on to skewers and grill or barbecue over low coals for 15 minutes, basting with the marinade and turning frequently. Serve garnished with extra mint and citrus slices if desired.

Chicken Satay

Marinate in the satay sauce overnight to allow the flavours to penetrate the chicken. Soak wooden skewers in water overnight to prevent them from burning while cooking.

INGREDIENTS

Serves 4

4 chicken breasts

lemon slices, to garnish

lettuce leaves, to serve

spring onions, to serve

For the satay

115g/4oz/^{1}/$_2$ cup crunchy peanut butter

1 small onion, chopped

1 garlic clove, crushed

30ml/2 tbsp chutney

60ml/4 tbsp olive oil

5ml/1 tsp light soy sauce

30ml/2 tbsp lemon juice

1.5ml/^{1}/$_4$ tsp chilli powder or cayenne

   pepper

1 Put all the satay ingredients into a food processor or blender and process until smooth. Spoon into a large dish.

2 Remove all bone and skin from the chicken and cut into 2.5cm/1in cubes. Add to the satay mixture and stir to coat the chicken pieces. Cover with clear film and chill for at least 4 hours or, better still, overnight.

3 Preheat the grill or barbecue. Thread the chicken pieces on to the satay sticks.

4 Cook for 10 minutes, brushing occasionally with the satay sauce. Serve on a bed of lettuce with spring onions and garnish with lemon slices.

Chicken and Pasta Salad

This is a delicious way to use up leftover cooked chicken.

INGREDIENTS

Serves 4

225g/8oz/2 cups tri-coloured pasta twists

30ml/2 tbsp pesto sauce

15ml/1 tbsp olive oil

1 beefsteak tomato

12 stoned black olives

225g/8oz/1^{1}/2 cups cooked French beans

350g/12oz/3 cups cooked chicken, cubed

salt and black pepper

fresh basil, to garnish

1 Cook the pasta in plenty of boiling, salted water until al dente (about 12 minutes or as directed on the packet).

2 Drain the pasta and rinse in plenty of cold running water. Put into a bowl and stir in the pesto sauce and olive oil.

3 Skin the tomato by placing in boiling water for about 10 seconds and then into cold water, to loosen the skin.

4 Cut the tomato into small cubes and add to the pasta with the olives, seasoning and French beans cut into 4cm/1^{1}/2in lengths. Add the cubed chicken. Toss gently together and transfer to a serving platter. Garnish with fresh basil.

Barbecued Jerk Chicken

Jerk refers to the blend of herb and spice seasoning rubbed into meat, before it is roasted over charcoal sprinkled with pimiento berries. In Jamaica, jerk seasoning was originally used only for pork, but jerked chicken is equally good.

INGREDIENTS

Serves 4

8 chicken pieces

For the marinade

5ml/1 tsp ground allspice

5ml/1 tsp ground cinnamon

5ml/1 tsp dried thyme

1.5ml/$\frac{1}{4}$ tsp freshly grated nutmeg

10ml/2 tsp demerara sugar

2 garlic cloves, crushed

15ml/1 tbsp finely chopped onion

15ml/1 tbsp chopped spring onion

15ml/1 tbsp vinegar

30ml/2 tbsp oil

15ml/1 tbsp lime juice

1 hot chilli pepper, chopped

salt and black pepper

salad leaves, to serve

1 Combine all the marinade ingredients in a small bowl. Using a fork, mash them together well to form a thick paste.

2 Lay the chicken pieces on a plate or board and make several lengthways slits in the flesh. Rub the seasoning all over the chicken and into the slits.

3 Place the chicken pieces in a dish, cover with clear film and marinate overnight in the fridge. Shake off any excess seasoning from the chicken. Brush with oil and place either on a baking sheet if cooking inside or on a barbecue grill if barbecuing.

4 Cook under a preheated grill for 45 minutes, turning often. Or, if barbecuing, light the coals and when ready, cook over the coals for 30 minutes, turning often. Serve hot with salad leaves.

COOK'S TIP

The flavour is best if you marinate the chicken overnight.

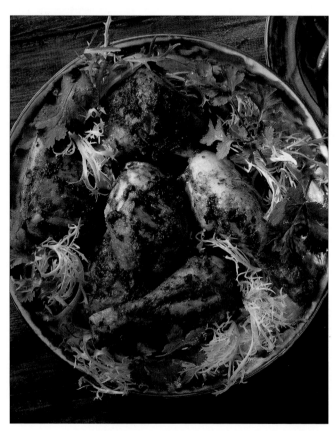

Grilled Spatchcocked Poussins

Grilled poussins with an onion and herb dressing.

INGREDIENTS

Serves 4

4 poussins, about 450g/1lb each,
    spatchcocked
olive oil
salt and black pepper

For the onion and herb sauce
30ml/2 tbsp dry sherry
30ml/2 tbsp lemon juice
30ml/2 tbsp olive oil
50g/2oz spring onions, chopped
1 garlic clove, finely chopped
60ml/4 tbsp chopped mixed fresh herbs
    such as tarragon, parsley, thyme,
    marjoram, lemon balm

1 Preheat the grill to high, or
prepare a charcoal barbecue.

2 Season the spatchcocked birds,
then brush them with a little
olive oil. Set them on the rack in
the grill pan, about 10cm/4in from
the heat, or on the barbecue
15cm/6in above the coals.

3 Cook for 20–25 minutes or
until tender. Turn and brush
with more oil halfway through the
cooking time.

4 Meanwhile, to make the sauce,
whisk together the sherry,
lemon juice, olive oil, spring
onions and garlic. Season with salt
and pepper.

5 When the poussins are done,
transfer them to a deep serving
platter. Whisk the herbs into the
sauce, then spoon it over the birds.
Cover tightly with another platter
or with foil and leave to rest for
15 minutes before serving.

Chinese-style Chicken Salad

Shredded chicken is served with a tasty peanut sauce.

INGREDIENTS

Serves 4

4 boneless chicken breasts, about
    175g/6oz each

60ml/4 tbsp dark soy sauce

pinch of Chinese five-spice powder

a good squeeze of lemon juice

$1/2$ cucumber, peeled and cut into
    matchsticks

5ml/1 tsp salt

45ml/3 tbsp sunflower oil

30ml/2 tbsp sesame oil

15ml/1 tbsp sesame seeds

30ml/2 tbsp dry sherry

2 carrots, cut into matchsticks

8 spring onions, shredded

75g/3oz/$1/2$ cup beansprouts

For the sauce

60ml/4 tbsp crunchy peanut butter

10ml/2 tsp lemon juice

10ml/2 tsp sesame oil

1.5ml/$1/4$ tsp hot chilli powder

1 spring onion, finely chopped

1 Put the chicken portions into a large pan and just cover with water. Add 15ml/1 tbsp of the soy sauce, the Chinese five-spice powder and lemon juice, cover and bring to the boil, then simmer for about 20 minutes.

2 Place the cucumber match-sticks in a colander, sprinkle with the salt and cover with a weighted plate. Leave to drain for 30 minutes.

3 Heat the oils in a large frying pan or wok. Add the sesame seeds, fry for 30 seconds and then stir in the remaining soy sauce and the sherry. Add the carrots and stir-fry for 2–3 minutes. Remove and reserve.

4 Remove the chicken from the pan and leave until cool enough to handle. Discard the skins and bash the chicken lightly with a rolling pin to loosen the fibres. Slice in strips and reserve.

5 Rinse the cucumber well, pat dry with kitchen paper and place in a bowl. Add the spring onions, beansprouts, cooked carrots, pan juices and shredded chicken, and mix together. Transfer to a shallow dish. Cover and chill for about 1 hour, turning the mixture in the juices once or twice.

6 To make the sauce, cream the peanut butter with the lemon juice, sesame oil and chilli powder, adding a little hot water to form a paste, then stir in the spring onion. Arrange the chicken mixture on a serving dish and serve with the peanut butter.

Fusilli with Chicken, Tomatoes and Broccoli

This is a really hearty main-course salad for a hungry family.

INGREDIENTS

Serves 4

675g/1¹/₂lb ripe but firm plum tomatoes, quartered
90ml/6 tbsp olive oil
5ml/1 tsp dried oregano
salt and black pepper
350g/12oz broccoli florets
1 small onion, sliced
5ml/1 tsp dried thyme
450g/1lb/3 cups chicken breast, boned, skinned and cubed
3 garlic cloves, crushed
15ml/1 tbsp fresh lemon juice
450g/1lb fusilli pasta

1 Preheat the oven to 200°C/400°F/Gas 6.

2 Place the tomatoes in a baking dish. Add 15ml/1 tbsp of the oil, the oregano, and 5ml/¹/₂ tsp salt and stir to blend.

3 Bake until the tomatoes are just browned, about 30–40 minutes; do not stir.

4 Meanwhile, bring a large pan of salted water to the boil. Add the broccoli and cook until just tender, about 5 minutes. Drain and set aside. (Alternatively, steam the broccoli until tender.)

5 Heat 30ml/2 tbsp of the oil in a large non-stick frying pan. Add the onion, thyme, chicken cubes and 2.5ml/¹/₂ tsp salt. Cook over high heat, stirring often, until the meat is cooked and beginning to brown, 5–7 minutes. Add the garlic and cook 1 minute more, stirring.

6 Remove from the heat. Stir in the lemon juice and season with pepper. Keep warm until the pasta is cooked.

7 Bring another large pan of salted water to the boil. Add the fusilli and cook until just tender (check the instructions on the packet for timing). Drain and place in a large bowl. Toss with the remaining oil.

8 Add the broccoli to the chicken mixture. Add to the fusilli. Add the tomatoes and stir gently to blend. Serve immediately.

Swiss Cheese, Chicken and Tongue Salad

The rich sweet flavours of this salad marry well with the peppery watercress. A minted lemon dressing freshens the overall effect. Serve with new potatoes.

INGREDIENTS

Serves 4

2 free-range chicken breasts, skinned and boned

$^{1}/_{2}$ chicken stock cube

225g/8oz sliced ox tongue or ham, 5mm/$^{1}/_{4}$in thick

225g/8oz Gruyère cheese

1 lollo rosso lettuce

1 butterhead or Batavian endive lettuce

1 bunch watercress

2 green-skinned apples, cored and sliced

3 sticks celery, sliced

60ml/4 tbsp sesame seeds, toasted

salt, black pepper and nutmeg

Dressing

75ml/5 tbsp groundnut or sunflower oil

5ml/1 tsp sesame oil

45ml/3 tbsp lemon juice

10ml/2 tsp chopped fresh mint

3 drops Tabasco sauce

1 Place the chicken breasts in a shallow saucepan, cover with 300ml/$^{1}/_{2}$ pint/1$^{1}/_{4}$ cups water, add the $^{1}/_{2}$ stock cube and bring to the boil. Put the lid on the pan and simmer for 15 minutes. Drain, reserving the stock for another occasion, then cool the chicken under cold running water.

2 To make the dressing, measure the two oils, lemon juice, mint and Tabasco sauce into a screw-top jar and shake. Cut the chicken, tongue and Gruyère cheese into fine strips. Moisten with a little dressing and set aside.

3 Combine the salad leaves with the apple and celery, and dress. Distribute among 4 large plates. Pile the chicken, tongue and cheese in the centre, scatter with toasted sesame seeds, season with salt, pepper and freshly grated nutmeg and serve.

Chicken Liver, Bacon and Tomato Salad

Warm salads are especially welcome during the autumn months when the evenings are growing shorter and cooler. Try this rich salad with sweet spinach and bitter leaves of frisée lettuce.

INGREDIENTS

Serves 4

225g/8oz young spinach, stems removed

1 frisée lettuce

105ml/7 tbsp groundnut or sunflower oil

175g/6oz rindless unsmoked bacon, cut into strips

75g/3oz day-old bread, crusts removed and cut into short fingers

450g/1lb chicken livers

115g/4oz cherry tomatoes

salt and black pepper

1 Place the salad leaves in a salad bowl. Heat 60ml/4 tbsp of the oil in a large frying pan. Add the bacon and cook for 3–4 minutes or until crisp and brown. Remove the bacon with a slotted spoon and drain on a piece of kitchen paper.

2 To make the croûtons, fry the bread in the bacon-flavoured oil, tossing until crisp and golden. Drain on kitchen paper.

3 Heat the remaining 45ml/ 3 tbsp of oil in the frying pan, add the chicken livers and fry briskly for 2–3 minutes. Turn out over the salad leaves, add the bacon, croûtons and tomatoes. Season, toss and serve.

Wild Rice and Chicken Salad

Once you have cooked the wild rice, this is a very simple salad to make.

Serves 4

175g/6oz/1 cup dry weight wild rice,
   boiled or steamed
2 celery sticks, thinly sliced
50g/2oz spring onions, chopped
115g/4oz/1$\frac{1}{2}$ cups small button
   mushrooms, quartered
450g/1lb cooked chicken breast, diced
120ml/4 fl oz/$\frac{1}{2}$ cup vinaigrette dressing
5ml/1 tsp fresh thyme leaves
2 pears, peeled, halved and cored
25g/1oz/$\frac{1}{4}$ cup walnut pieces, toasted

1 Combine cooled cooked wild rice with the celery, spring onions, mushrooms and chicken in a bowl.

2 Add the dressing and thyme; toss well together.

3 Thinly slice the pear halves lengthways without cutting through the stalk end and spread the slices into a fan. Divide the salad among 4 plates. Garnish each with a fanned pear half and walnuts.

COOKING WILD RICE

To boil: Add the rice to a large pot of boiling salted water (about four parts water to each one of rice). Bring back to a gentle boil and cook for 45–50 minutes or until the rice is tender but still firm and has begun to split open. Drain well.
To steam: Put the rice in a saucepan with the measured quantity of salted water. Bring to the boil, cover and steam over very low heat for 45–50 minutes or until tender. Cook uncovered for the last 5 minutes to evaporate excess water.

Warm Chicken Liver Salad

Although warm salads may seem over-fussy or trendy, there are times when they are just right. Serve this delicious combination as either a starter or a light meal, with hunks of bread to dip into the dressing.

INGREDIENTS

Serves 4

115g/4oz each fresh young spinach leaves,
    rocket and lollo rosso lettuce
2 pink grapefruit
90ml/6 tbsp sunflower oil
10ml/2 tsp sesame oil
10ml/2 tsp soy sauce
225g/8oz chicken livers, chopped
salt and black pepper

1 Wash, dry and tear up all the leaves. Mix them together well in a large salad bowl.

2 Carefully cut away all the peel and white pith from the grapefruit, then segment them saving the juice. Add the grapefruit to the salad leaves.

3 To make the dressing, mix together 60ml/4 tbsp of the sunflower oil with the sesame oil, soy sauce, seasoning and grapefruit juice to taste.

4 Heat the rest of the sunflower oil in a small pan and cook the liver, stirring gently, until firm and lightly browned.

5 Tip the chicken livers and dressing over the salad and serve at once.

COOK'S TIP

Chicken or turkey livers are ideal for this recipe, and there's no need to leave them to defrost completely before cooking.

Orange Chicken Salad

A refreshing and very delicately flavoured rice salad.

Serves 4

3 large seedless oranges

175g/6oz/1 cup long grain rice

475ml/16fl oz/2 cups water

175ml/6fl oz/^{3}/4 cup vinaigrette dressing, made with red wine vinegar and a mixture of olive and vegetable oils

10ml/2 tsp Dijon mustard

2.5ml/^{1}/2 tsp caster sugar

450g/1lb/3 cups cooked chicken, diced

45ml/3 tbsp snipped chives

75g/3oz/^{1}/2 cup roasted cashew nuts

salt and black pepper

cucumber slices, to garnish

1 Thinly peel 1 orange, taking only the coloured part of the rind and leaving the white pith.

2 Combine the orange rind, rice and water in a saucepan. Add a pinch of salt. Bring to the boil, then cover and steam over very low heat for 15–18 minutes or until the rice is tender and all the water has been absorbed.

3 Peel the remaining oranges and cut out the segments, reserving the juice. Add the orange juice to the vinaigrette dressing. Add the mustard and sugar and whisk to combine well. Taste and add more salt and pepper if needed.

4 When the rice is cooked, remove it from the heat and cool slightly, uncovered. Discard the orange rind.

5 Turn the rice into a bowl and add half of the dressing. Toss well and cool completely.

6 Add the chicken, chives, cashew nuts and orange segments to the rice with the remaining dressing. Toss gently. Serve at room temperature, garnished with cucumber.

Making Vinaigrette Dressing

A good vinaigrette can do more than dress a salad. It can also be used to baste meat, poultry, seafood or vegetables during cooking; and it can be used as a flavouring and tenderising marinade. The basic mixture of oil, vinegar and seasoning lends itself to many variations.

Vinaigrette dressing will keep in the fridge, in a tightly sealed container, for several weeks. Add flavourings, particularly fresh herbs, just before using.

Makes just over 175ml/6 fl oz/^{3}/4 cup

45ml/3 tbsp wine vinegar

salt and pepper

150ml/^{1}/4 pint/^{2}/3 cup vegetable oil

1 Put the vinegar, salt and pepper in a bowl and whisk to dissolve the salt. Gradually add the oil, stirring with the whisk. Taste and adjust seasoning.

Grilled Chicken Salad with Lavender

Lavender may seem like an odd salad ingredient, but its delightful scent has a natural affinity with sweet garlic, orange and other wild herbs. A serving of polenta makes this salad both filling and delicious.

INGREDIENTS

Serves 4

4 chicken breasts, boned

900ml/1¹/₂ pints/3³/₄ cups light chicken
   stock

175g/6oz/1 cup fine polenta

50g/2oz/4tbsp butter

450g/1lb young spinach

175g/6oz lamb's lettuce

8 sprigs fresh lavender

8 small tomatoes, halved

salt and black pepper

Lavender Marinade

6 fresh lavender flowers

10ml/2 tsp finely grated orange rind

2 cloves garlic, crushed

10ml/2 tsp clear honey

salt

30ml/2 tbsp olive oil

10ml/2 tsp chopped fresh thyme

10ml/2 tsp chopped fresh marjoram

1 To make the marinade, strip the lavender flowers from the stems and combine with the orange rind, garlic, honey and salt. Add the olive oil and herbs. Slash the chicken deeply, spread the mixture over the chicken and leave to marinate in a cool place for at least 20 minutes.

2 To cook the polenta, bring the chicken stock to the boil in a heavy saucepan. Add the polenta in a steady stream, stirring all the time until thick: this will take 2–3 minutes. Turn the cooked polenta out on to a 2.5cm/1in deep buttered tray and allow to cool.

3 Heat the grill to a moderate temperature. (If using a barbecue, let the embers settle to a steady glow.) Grill the chicken for about 15 minutes, turning once.

4 Cut the polenta into 2.5cm/1in cubes with a wet knife. Heat the butter in a large frying pan and fry the polenta until golden.

5 Wash the salad leaves and spin dry, then divide among 4 large plates. Slice each chicken breast and lay over the salad. Place the polenta among the salad, decorate with sprigs of lavender and tomatoes, season and serve.

Maryland Salad

Barbecue-grilled chicken, sweetcorn, bacon, banana and watercress combine here in a sensational main-course salad. Serve with jacket potatoes and a knob of butter.

INGREDIENTS

Serves 4

4 chicken breasts, boned
225g/8oz rindless unsmoked bacon
4 corn on the cob
45ml/3 tbsp butter, softened
4 ripe bananas, peeled and halved
4 firm tomatoes, halved
1 escarole or butterhead lettuce
1 bunch watercress
salt and black pepper

For the dressing

75ml/5 tbsp groundnut oil
15ml/1 tbsp white wine vinegar
10ml/2 tsp maple syrup
10ml/2 tsp mild mustard

1 Season the chicken breasts, brush with oil and barbecue or grill for 15 minutes, turning once. Barbecue or grill the bacon for 8–10 minutes, or until crisp.

2 Bring a large saucepan of salted water to the boil. Shuck and trim the corn cobs. Boil for 20 minutes. For extra flavour, brush with butter and brown over the barbecue or under the grill. Barbecue or grill the bananas and tomatoes for 6–8 minutes, brush these with butter too if you wish.

3 To make the dressing, combine the oil, vinegar, maple syrup and mustard with seasoning and 15ml/1 tbsp water in a screw-top jar and shake well.

4 Wash, spin thoroughly and dress the salad leaves.

5 Distribute the salad leaves among 4 large plates. Slice the chicken and arrange over the leaves with the bacon, banana, sweetcorn and tomatoes.

Grilled Chicken with Pica de Gallo Salsa

This dish originates from Mexico. Its hot fruity flavours form the essence of Tex-Mex cooking.

INGREDIENTS

Serves 4

4 chicken breasts

pinch of celery salt and cayenne pepper combined

30ml/2 tbsp vegetable oil

corn chips, to serve

For the salsa

275g/10oz watermelon

175g/6oz canteloupe melon

1 small red onion

1–2 green chillies

30ml/2 tbsp lime juice

60ml/4 tbsp chopped fresh coriander

pinch of salt

1 Preheat a moderate grill. Slash the chicken breasts deeply to speed up the cooking time.

2 Season the chicken with celery salt and cayenne, brush with oil and grill for about 15 minutes.

3 To make the salsa, remove the rind and as many seeds as you can from the melons. Finely dice the flesh and put it into a bowl.

4 Finely chop the onion, split the chillies (discarding the seeds which contain most of the heat) and chop. Take care when handling cut chillies. Mix with the melon.

5 Add the lime juice and coriander, and season with salt. Turn the salsa into a small bowl.

6 Arrange the grilled chicken on a plate and serve with the salsa and a handful of corn chips.

COOK'S TIP

To capture the spirit of Tex-Mex food, cook the chicken over a barbecue and eat shaded from the hot summer sun.

Coronation Chicken

A summer favourite – serve with a crisp green salad.

INGREDIENTS

Serves 8

¹/₂ lemon

2.25kg/5–5¹/₄lb chicken

1 onion, quartered

1 carrot, quartered

large bouquet garni

8 black peppercorns, crushed

salt

watercress sprigs, to garnish

For the sauce

1 small onion, chopped

15g/¹/₂oz/1 tbsp butter

15ml/1 tbsp curry paste

15ml/1 tbsp tomato purée

120ml/4fl oz/¹/₂ cup red wine

bay leaf

juice of ¹/₂ lemon, or more to taste

10–15ml/2–3 tsp apricot jam

300ml/¹/₂ pint/1¹/₄ cups mayonnaise

120ml/4fl oz/¹/₂ cup whipping cream, whipped

salt and black pepper

1 Put the lemon half in the chicken cavity, then place the chicken in a saucepan that it just fits. Add the vegetables, bouquet garni, peppercorns and salt.

3 Transfer the chicken to a large bowl, pour over the cooking liquid and leave to cool. Skin, bone, then chop the chicken flesh.

5 Beat the sauce into the mayonnaise. Fold in the whipped cream. Add seasoning, then stir in the chicken and garnish with watercress.

2 Add sufficient water to come two-thirds of the way up the chicken, bring to the boil, then cover and cook gently for 1¹/₂ hours, until the juices run clear.

4 To make the sauce, cook the onion in the butter until soft. Add the curry paste, tomato purée, wine, bay leaf and lemon juice, then cook for 10 minutes. Add the apricot jam; sieve and cool.

Peanut Chicken in Pineapple Boats

An impressive looking dish to serve at a dinner party.

Serves 4

2 small ripe pineapples

225g/8 oz/1¹/2 cups cooked chicken
    breast, cut into bite-size pieces

2 celery sticks, diced

50g/2oz spring onions, white and green
    parts, chopped

225g/8oz seedless green grapes

40g/1¹/2 oz salted peanuts, coarsely
    chopped

Dressing

75g/3oz smooth peanut butter

120ml/4 fl oz/¹/2 cup mayonnaise

30ml/2 tbsp cream or milk

1 garlic clove, finely chopped

5ml/1 tsp mild curry powder

15ml/1tbsp apricot jam

salt and black pepper

1 Make 4 pineapple boats from
the pineapples. Cut the flesh
removed from the boats into
bite-size pieces.

2 Combine the pineapple flesh,
chicken, celery, spring onions
and grapes in a bowl.

3 Put all the dressing ingredients
in another bowl and mix with a
wooden spoon or whisk until
evenly blended. Season with salt
and pepper. (The dressing will be
thick, but will be thinned by the
juices from the pineapple.)

4 Add the dressing to the
pineapple and chicken
mixture. Fold together gently but
thoroughly.

5 Divide the chicken salad
among the pineapple boats.
Sprinkle the peanuts over the top
before serving.

Warm Chicken and Coriander Salad

This salad needs to be served warm to make the most of the wonderful sesame and coriander flavourings. It makes a simple starter or a delicious light lunch dish.

Serves 6

4 medium chicken breasts, boned and
   skinned
225g/8oz mange-touts
2 heads decorative lettuce such as lollo
   rosso or oakleaf
3 carrots, peeled and cut into small
   matchsticks
175g/6oz/2³/4 cups button mushrooms,
   sliced
6 rashers of bacon, fried and chopped
1 tbsp chopped fresh coriander leaves,
   to garnish

Dressing

120ml/4fl oz/¹/2 cup lemon juice
30ml/2 tbsp wholegrain mustard
250ml/8fl oz/1 cup olive oil
60ml/4 tbsp sesame oil
1 tsp coriander seeds, crushed

1 Mix all the dressing ingredients in a bowl. Place the chicken breasts in a shallow dish and pour on half the dressing. Chill overnight, and store the remaining dressing in the fridge.

2 Cook the mange-touts for 2 minutes in boiling water, then cool under running cold water to stop them cooking any further. Tear the lettuces into small pieces and mix the other salad ingredients and the bacon together. Arrange all these in individual serving dishes.

3 Grill the chicken breasts until cooked through, then slice them on the diagonal into quite thin pieces. Divide among the bowls of salad, and add some dressing to each dish. Combine quickly and scatter some fresh coriander over each bowl.

Sweet and Sour Kebabs

This marinade contains sugar and will burn very easily, so grill the kebabs slowly, turning often. Serve with Harlequin Rice.

INGREDIENTS

Serves 4

2 chicken breasts, boned and skinned

8 pickling onions or 2 medium onions, peeled

4 rindless streaky bacon rashers

3 firm bananas

1 red pepper, seeded and sliced

For the marinade

30ml/2 tbsp soft brown sugar

15ml/1 tbsp Worcestershire sauce

30ml/2 tbsp lemon juice

salt and black pepper

For the Harlequin Rice

30ml/2 tbsp olive oil

225g/8oz/generous 1 cup cooked rice

115g/4oz/1 cup cooked peas

1 small red pepper, seeded and diced

1 Mix together the marinade ingredients. Cut each chicken breast into four pieces, add to the marinade, cover and leave for at least 4 hours or preferably overnight in the fridge.

2 Peel the pickling onions, blanch them in boiling water for 5 minutes and drain. If using medium onions, quarter them after blanching.

3 Cut each rasher of bacon in half. Peel the bananas and cut each into three pieces. Wrap a rasher of bacon around each piece of banana.

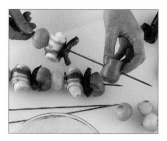

4 Thread on to metal skewers with the chicken pieces, onions and pepper slices. Brush with the marinade.

5 Grill or barbecue over low coals for 15 minutes, turning and basting frequently with the marinade. Keep warm while you prepare the rice.

6 Heat the oil in a frying pan and add the rice, peas and diced pepper. Stir until heated through and serve with the kebabs.

Chicken and Fruit Salad

The chickens may be cooked a day before eating and the salad can be quickly put together for lunch.

Serves 8

4 sprigs tarragon or rosemary

2 x 1.75kg/4lb chickens

65g/2^1/$_2$oz/5 tbsp softened butter

150ml/^{1}/$_4$ pint/^{2}/$_3$ cup chicken stock

150ml/^{1}/$_4$ pint/^{2}/$_3$ cup white wine

115g/4oz/1 cup walnut pieces

1 small cantaloupe melon

lettuce leaves

450g/1lb seedless grapes or stoned
  cherries

salt and black pepper

Dressing

30ml/2 tbsp tarragon vinegar

120ml/4 fl oz/^{1}/$_2$ cup light olive oil

30ml/2 tbsp chopped mixed fresh herbs,
  e.g. parsley, mint and tarragon

1 Preheat the oven to 200°C/400°F/Gas 6. Put the herb sprigs inside the chickens and season. Tie the chickens with string. Spread the chickens with 50g/2oz/4 tbsp of the softened butter, place in a roasting tin and pour round the stock. Cover loosely with foil and roast for about 1^1/2 hours, basting twice, until browned and the juices run clear. Remove the chickens from the roasting tin.

2 Add the wine to the roasting tin. Bring to the boil and cook until syrupy. Strain and leave to cool. Heat the remaining butter in a frying pan and gently fry the walnuts until browned. Drain and cool. Scoop the melon into balls or into cubes, joint the chickens.

3 To make the dressing, whisk the vinegar and oil together with a little salt and freshly ground black pepper. Remove all the fat from the chicken juices and add these to the dressing with the herbs. Adjust the seasoning.

4 Arrange the chicken pieces on a bed of lettuce, scatter over the grapes or stoned cherries, melon balls or cubes and spoon over the herb dressing. Sprinkle with toasted walnuts.

Warm Stir-fried Salad

Warm salads are becoming increasingly popular because they are delicious and nutritious. Arrange the salad leaves on four individual plates, so the hot stir-fry can be served straight from the wok, ensuring the lettuce remains crisp and the chicken warm.

INGREDIENTS

Serves 4

15ml/1 tbsp fresh tarragon
2 chicken breasts, about 225g/8oz each, boned and skinned
5cm/2in piece fresh root ginger, peeled and finely chopped
45ml/3 tbsp light soy sauce
15ml/1 tbsp sugar
15ml/1 tbsp sunflower oil
1 head Chinese lettuce
1/2 frisée lettuce, torn into bite-size pieces
115g/4oz/1 cup unsalted cashew nuts
2 large carrots, peeled and cut into fine strips
salt and black pepper

1 Chop the fresh tarragon. Cut the chicken into fine strips and place in a bowl.

2 To make the marinade, mix together in a bowl the tarragon, ginger, soy sauce, sugar and seasoning.

3 Pour the marinade over the chicken strips and leave to marinate for 2–4 hours.

4 Strain the chicken from the marinade, reserving the liquid. Heat a wok or large frying pan, then add the oil. When the oil is hot, stir-fry the chicken for 3 minutes, add the marinade and bubble for 2–3 minutes.

5 Slice the Chinese lettuce and arrange on a plate with the frisée. Toss the cashews and carrots together with the chicken and sauce, pile on top of the bed of lettuce and serve immediately.

Indonesian-style Satay Chicken

*Use boneless chicken thighs to give a
good flavour to these satays.*

Serves 4

50g/2oz/¹/2 cup raw peanuts

45ml/3 tbsp vegetable oil

small onion, finely chopped

2.5cm/1in piece fresh root ginger, peeled
    and finely chopped

1 clove garlic, crushed

675g/1¹/2lb chicken thighs, skinned and
    cut into cubes

130g/3¹/2oz creamed coconut, roughly
    chopped

15ml/1 tbsp chilli sauce

60ml/2fl oz/¹/4 cup crunchy peanut butter

5ml/1 tsp soft dark brown sugar

150ml/¹/4 pint/²/3 cup milk

1.5ml/¹/4 tsp salt

1 Shell and rub the skins from
the peanuts, then soak them in
a bowl with enough water to cover
them, for 1 minute. Drain the
peanuts and carefully cut them
into fine slivers.

2 Heat a wok or large frying pan
and add 5ml/1 tsp of the oil.
When the oil is hot, stir-fry the
peanuts for 1 minute until crisp
and golden. Remove them with
a slotted spoon and drain on
kitchen paper.

3 Add the remaining oil to the
hot wok. When the oil is hot,
add the onion, ginger and garlic
and stir-fry for 2–3 minutes until
softened but not browned. Remove
and drain on kitchen paper.

4 Add the chicken and stir-fry
for 3–4 minutes until crisp on
all sides.

5 Thread on to pre-soaked
bamboo skewers and keep
warm in a low oven.

6 Add the creamed coconut to
the hot wok in small pieces and
stir-fry until melted. Add the chilli
sauce, peanut butter and cooked
onion, ginger and garlic, and
simmer for 2 minutes. Stir in the
sugar, milk and salt and simmer
for a further 3 minutes. Serve the
skewered chicken hot, with a dash
of the hot dipping sauce sprinkled
with the peanuts.

PASTRIES
& PIES

Curried Chicken and Apricot Pie

This pie is unusually sweet-sour and very more-ish. Use boneless turkey instead of chicken, if you wish.

Serves 6

30ml/2 tbsp sunflower oil

1 large onion, chopped

450g/1lb chicken, boned and roughly chopped

15ml/1 tbsp curry paste or powder

30ml/2 tbsp apricot or peach chutney

115g/4oz/¹/₂ cup ready-to-eat dried apricots, halved

115g/4oz cooked carrots, sliced

5ml/1 tsp mixed dried herbs

60ml/4 tbsp crème fraîche

350g/12oz ready-made shortcrust pastry

little egg or milk, to glaze

salt and black pepper

3 Roll out the pastry to 2.5cm/ 1in wider than the pie dish. Cut a strip of pastry from the edge. Damp the rim of the dish, press on the strip, then brush with water and place the sheet of pastry on top, press to seal.

4 Preheat the oven to 190°C/ 375°F/Gas 5. Trim off any excess pastry and use to make an attractive pattern on the top if you wish. Brush all over with beaten egg or milk and bake for 40 minutes, until crisp and golden.

1 Heat the oil in a large pan and fry the onion and chicken until just colouring. Add the curry paste or powder and fry for another 2 minutes.

2 Add the chutney, apricots, carrots, herbs and crème fraîche to the pan with seasoning. Mix well and then transfer to a deep 900ml–1.2 litre/1¹/₂–2 pint/ 4–5 cup pie dish.

Chicken Parcels with Herb Butter

A herb-coated, buttery chicken fillet wrapped up in crisp pastry.

INGREDIENTS

Serves 4

4 chicken breast fillets, skinned

150g/5oz/³/4 cup butter, softened

90ml/6 tbsp chopped mixed fresh herbs,
    such as thyme, parsley, oregano and
    rosemary

5ml/1 tsp lemon juice

5 large sheets filo pastry, defrosted if
    frozen

1 egg, beaten

30ml/2 tbsp grated Parmesan cheese

salt and black pepper

1 Season the chicken fillets and fry in 25g/1oz/2 tbsp of the butter to seal and brown lightly. Allow to cool.

2 Preheat the oven to 190°C/375°F/Gas 5. Put the remaining butter, the herbs, lemon juice and seasoning in a food processor and process until smooth. Melt half the herb butter.

3 Take one sheet of filo pastry and brush with herb butter. Cover the rest of the pastry with a damp dish towel. Fold the pastry sheet in half and brush again with butter. Place a chicken fillet about 2.5cm/1in from the top end.

4 Dot the chicken with a quarter of the remaining herb butter. Fold in the sides of the pastry, then roll up to enclose it completely. Place seam-side down on a lightly greased baking sheet. Repeat with the other chicken fillets.

5 Brush the filo parcels with beaten egg. Cut the last sheet of filo into strips, then scrunch and arrange on top. Brush the parcels once again with the egg glaze, then sprinkle with Parmesan cheese. Bake for about 35–40 minutes, until golden brown. Serve hot.

Kotopitta

This is based on a Greek chicken pie.
Serve hot or cold with a typical
Greek salad made from tomatoes,
cucumber, onions and feta cheese.

Serves 4

275g/10oz filo pastry
30ml/2 tbsp olive oil
75g/3oz/^{1}/2 cup chopped toasted
  almonds
30ml/2 tbsp milk

For the filling
15ml/1 tbsp olive oil
1 medium onion, finely chopped
1 garlic clove, crushed
450g/1lb cooked chicken, boned
50g/2oz/^{1}/4 cup feta cheese,
  crumbled
2 eggs, beaten
15ml/1 tbsp chopped fresh parsley
15ml/1 tbsp chopped fresh coriander
15ml/1 tbsp chopped fresh mint
salt and black pepper

1 To make the filling, heat the oil
in a large frying pan and cook
the chopped onion gently until
tender. Add the crushed garlic and
cook for a further 2 minutes.
Transfer to a bowl.

2 Remove the skin from the
chicken and mince or chop
finely. Add to the onion with the
rest of the filling ingredients. Mix
thoroughly and season with salt
and freshly ground black pepper.

3 Preheat the oven to 190°C/
375°F/Gas 5. Have a damp
dish towel ready to keep the filo
pastry covered at all times. You will
need to work fast, as the pastry
dries out very quickly when
exposed to air. Unravel the pastry
and cut the whole batch into a
30cm/12in square.

4 Taking half the sheets (cover
the remainder), brush one
sheet with a little olive oil, lay it on
a well greased 1.35 litre/2^1/4 pint
ovenproof dish.

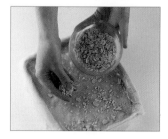

5 Sprinkle with a few almonds.
Repeat with the other pastry
sheets, overlapping them into the
dish. Spoon in the filling and cover
the pie in the same way with the
rest of the overlapping pastry.

6 Fold in the edges and mark a
diamond pattern on the
surface with a sharp knife. Brush
with milk and sprinkle on any
remaining almonds. Bake for
20–30 minutes or until golden.

Old-fashioned Chicken Pie

*The chicken can be roasted and the
sauce prepared a day in advance.
Leave to cool completely before
covering with pastry and baking.
Make into four individual pies if you
prefer but bake for 10 minutes less.*

Serves 4

1.5kg/3–3¹/2lb chicken

1 onion, quartered

1 sprig fresh tarragon or rosemary

25g/1oz/2 tbsp butter

115g/4oz/1¹/2 cups button mushrooms

30ml/2 tbsp plain flour

300ml/¹/2 pint/1¹/4 cups chicken stock

115g/4oz cooked ham, diced

30ml/2 tbsp chopped fresh parsley

450g/1lb ready-made puff or flaky pastry

1 egg, beaten

salt and black pepper

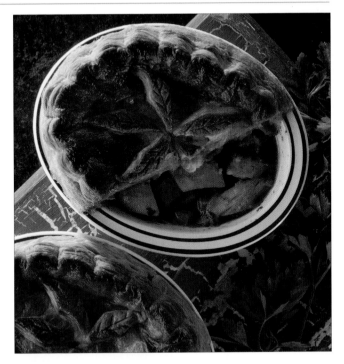

1 Preheat the oven to 200°C/
400°F/Gas 6. Put the chicken
into a casserole together with the
quartered onion and the herbs.
Add 300ml/¹/2 pint/1¹/4 cups water
and season. Cover and roast for
about 1¹/4 hours or until the
chicken is tender.

2 Remove the chicken and strain
the liquid into a measuring jug.
Cool and remove any fat that
settles on the surface. Make up to
300ml/¹/2 pint/1¹/4 cups with water
and reserve for the sauce.

3 Remove the chicken from the
bones and cut into large cubes.
Melt the butter in a pan, add the
mushrooms and cook for 2–3
minutes. Sprinkle in the flour and
gradually blend in the stock.

4 Bring to the boil, season to
taste and add the ham, chicken
and parsley. Turn into a large pie
dish and leave to cool.

5 Roll out the pastry on a lightly
floured surface to 5cm/2in
larger than the pie dish. Cut a
narrow strip of pastry to place
around the edge of the dish.
Dampen with a little water and
stick to the rim of the dish. Brush
the strip with beaten egg.

6 Lay the pastry loosely over the
pie, taking care not to stretch
it. Press firmly on to the rim. Using
a sharp knife, trim away the excess
pastry and knock up the sides to
encourage the pastry to rise.
Crimp the edge neatly and cut a
hole in the centre of the pie. This
allows steam to escape during
cooking. Decorate with pastry
leaves and chill until ready to bake.

7 Brush the pastry with beaten
egg (taking care not to glaze
over the sides of the pastry). Bake
in the oven for 35–45 minutes,
until well risen and nicely browned
all over.

Chicken and Mushroom Pie

Use a mixture of dried and fresh mushrooms for this pie.

Serves 6

15g/¹/₂oz/¹/₄ cup dried porcini
   mushrooms
50g/2oz/¹/₄ cup/4 tbsp butter
30ml/2 tbsp flour
250ml/8fl oz/1 cup chicken stock, warmed
50ml/2fl oz/¹/₄ cup whipping cream or
   milk
1 onion, coarsely chopped
2 carrots, sliced
2 celery sticks, coarsely chopped
50g/2oz/³/₄ cup fresh mushrooms,
   quartered
450g/1lb/3 cups cooked chicken meat,
   cubed
50g/2oz/¹/₂ cup shelled fresh or frozen
   peas
salt and black pepper
beaten egg, for glazing

For the crust
225g/8oz/2 cups flour
1.5ml/¹/₄ tsp salt
115g/4oz/¹/₂ cup cold butter, cut in pieces
50g/2oz/¹/₃ cup lard
60–120ml/4–8 tbsp iced water

1 To make the crust, sift the flour and salt into a bowl. Cut in the butter and lard until the mixture resembles breadcrumbs. Sprinkle with 6 tbsp iced water and mix until the dough holds together. Add a little more water, if necessary, 1 tbsp at a time.

2 Gather the dough into a ball and flatten into a disk. Wrap in greaseproof paper and chill at least 30 minutes.

3 Place the porcini mushrooms in a small bowl. Add hot water to cover and soak until soft, about 30 minutes. Lift out of the water with a slotted spoon to leave any grit behind and drain. Discard the soaking water.

4 Preheat the oven to 190°C/ 375°F/Gas 5.

5 Melt 25g/1oz/2 tbsp of the butter in a heavy saucepan. Whisk in the flour and cook until bubbling, whisking constantly. Add the warm stock and cook over medium heat, whisking, until the mixture boils. Cook 2–3 minutes more. Whisk in the cream or milk. Season with salt and pepper. Put to one side.

6 Heat the remaining butter in a large non-stick frying pan until foamy. Add the onion and carrots and cook until softened, about 5 minutes. Add the celery and fresh mushrooms and cook 5 minutes more. Stir in the chicken, peas, and drained porcini mushrooms.

7 Add the chicken mixture to the sauce and stir. Taste for seasoning. Transfer to a rectangular 2.5 litre/4 pints/10 cup baking dish.

8 Roll out the dough to about 3mm/¹/₈in thickness. Cut out a rectangle about 2.5cm/1in larger all around than the dish. Lay the rectangle of dough over the filling. Make a decorative crimped edge by pushing the index finger of one hand between the thumb and index finger of the other.

9 Cut several vents in the top crust to allow steam to escape. Brush with the egg to glaze.

10 Press together the dough trimmings, then roll out again. Cut into strips and lay them over the top crust. Glaze again. If desired, roll small balls of dough and set them in the "windows" in the lattice.

11 Bake until the top crust is browned, about 30 minutes. Serve the pie hot.

Chicken en Croûte

Chicken breasts, layered with herbs and orange-flavoured stuffing and wrapped in light puff pastry, make an impressive dish to serve at a dinner party.

INGREDIENTS

Serves 8

450g/1lb packet puff pastry
4 large chicken breasts, boned and skinned
1 egg, beaten

For the stuffing

115g/4oz/1 cup leeks, thinly sliced
50g/2oz/^{1}/$_3$ cup streaky bacon, chopped
25g/1oz/2 tbsp butter
115g/4oz/2 cups fresh white breadcrumbs
30ml/2 tbsp chopped fresh herbs, e.g.
   parsley, thyme, marjoram and chives
grated rind of 1 large orange
1 egg, beaten
salt and black pepper

1 To make the stuffing, cook the sliced leeks and bacon in the butter until soft. Put the bread-crumbs into a bowl with the mixed herbs and plenty of seasoning. Add the leeks, bacon and butter with the grated orange rind and bind together with the beaten egg. If the mixture is too dry and crumbly, you can stir in a little orange juice or chicken stock to bring it to a moist consistency.

2 Roll the pastry out to a large rectangle 30 x 40cm/12 x 16in. Trim the edges and reserve for decorating the top.

3 Place the chicken breasts between two pieces of clear film and flatten to a thickness of 5mm/^{1}/$_4$in with a rolling pin. Spread a third of the leek stuffing over the centre of the pastry. Lay two chicken breasts side-by-side on top of the stuffing. Cover the chicken breasts with another third of the stuffing, then repeat with the remaining chicken breasts and the rest of the stuffing.

4 Make a cut diagonally from each corner of the pastry to the chicken. Brush the pastry with beaten egg.

5 Bring up the sides and overlap them slightly. Trim away any excess pastry before folding the ends over like a parcel. Turn over on to a greased baking tray, so that the joins are underneath. Shape neatly and trim any excess pastry.

6 With a sharp knife, lightly criss-cross the pastry into a diamond pattern. Brush with beaten egg and cut leaves from the trimmings to decorate the top. Bake at 200°C/400°F/Gas 6 for 50–60 minutes or until well risen and golden brown on top.

Hampshire Farmhouse Flan

The lattice pastry topping makes this flan look extra special.

Serves 4

225g/8oz/2 cups wholemeal flour
50g/2oz/^{1}/4 cup butter, cubed
50g/2oz/^{1}/3 cup lard
5ml/1 tsp caraway seeds
15ml/1 tbsp oil
1 onion, chopped
1 garlic clove, crushed
225g/8oz/2 cups chopped cooked
    chicken
75g/3oz/1^1/2 cups watercress leaves,
    chopped
grated rind of ^{1}/2 small lemon
2 eggs, lightly beaten
175ml/6fl oz/^{3}/4 cup double cream
45ml/3 tbsp natural yogurt
a good pinch of grated nutmeg
45ml/3 tbsp grated Caerphilly cheese
beaten egg, to glaze
salt and black pepper

3 Roll out the pastry and use to line an 18 x 28cm/7 x 11in loose-based flan tin. Reserve the trimmings. Prick the base and chill for 20 minutes. Place a baking sheet in the oven and preheat to 200°C/400°F/Gas 6.

4 Heat the oil in a frying pan and sauté the onions and garlic for 5–8 minutes, until just softened. Remove from the heat and cool.

5 Line the pastry case with greaseproof paper and fill with baking beans. Bake for 10 minutes, then remove the paper and beans and cook for 5 minutes.

6 Mix the onions, garlic, chicken, watercress and lemon rind. Spoon into the flan case. Beat the eggs, cream, yogurt, nutmeg, cheese and seasoning and pour over.

7 Roll out the pastry trimmings and cut out 1cm/^{1}/2in strips. Brush with egg, then lay in a lattice over the flan. Press the ends on to the pastry edge. Bake for 35 minutes, until the top is golden.

1 Place the flour in a bowl with a pinch of salt. Add the butter and lard and rub into the flour with your fingertips until the mixture resembles breadcrumbs. (Alternatively, you can use a blender or food processor for this.)

2 Stir in the caraway seeds and 45ml/3 tbsp iced water and mix to a firm dough. Knead lightly on a floured surface until smooth.

Chicken Charter Pie

Since this dish comes from Cornwall, rich double cream is used in the filling.

INGREDIENTS

Serves 4

50g/2oz/4 tbsp butter
4 chicken legs
1 onion, finely chopped
150ml/^{1}/$_4$ pint/^{2}/$_3$ cup milk
150ml/^{1}/$_4$ pint/^{2}/$_3$ cup soured cream
4 spring onions, quartered
20g/^{3}/$_4$ oz fresh parsley, finely
   chopped
225g/8oz ready-made puff pastry
120ml/4fl oz/^{1}/$_2$ cup double cream
2 eggs, beaten, plus extra for glazing
salt and black pepper

1 Melt the butter in a heavy-based, shallow pan, then brown the chicken legs. Transfer them on to a plate.

2 Add the chopped onion to the pan and cook until softened but not browned. Stir the milk, soured cream, spring onions, parsley and seasoning into the pan, bring to the boil, then simmer for a couple of minutes.

3 Return the chicken to the pan with any juices, then cover tightly and cook very gently for about 30 minutes. Transfer the chicken and sauce mixture to a 1.2 litre/2 pints/5 cups pie dish and leave to cool.

4 Meanwhile, roll out the pastry until about 2cm/^{3}/$_4$in larger all round than the top of the pie dish. Leave the pastry to relax while the chicken is cooling.

5 Preheat the oven to 220°C/425°F/Gas 7. Cut off a narrow strip around the edge of the pastry, then place the strip on the edge of the pie dish. Moisten the strip, then cover the dish with the pastry. Press the edges together.

6 Make a hole in the centre of the pastry and insert a small funnel of foil. Brush the pastry with egg, then bake for 15–20 minutes.

7 Reduce the oven temperature to 180°C/350°F/Gas 4. Mix the double cream and eggs, then pour into the pie through the funnel. Shake the pie to distribute the cream, then return to the oven for 5–10 minutes. Remove from the oven and leave in a warm place for 5–10 minutes before serving, or cool completely if serving cold.

Chicken and Ham Pie

This domed double-crust pie is suitable for a cold buffet, for picnics or any packed meals.

INGREDIENTS

Serves 8

400g/14oz ready-made shortcrust
    pastry
800g/1³/4 lb chicken breasts
350g/12oz uncooked gammon
about 60ml/2fl oz/¹/4 cup double cream
6 spring onions, finely chopped
15ml/1 tbsp chopped fresh tarragon
10ml/2 tsp chopped fresh thyme
grated rind and juice of ¹/2 large lemon
5ml/1 tsp freshly ground mace
salt and black pepper
beaten egg or milk, to glaze

1 Preheat the oven to 190°C/ 375°F/Gas 5. Roll out one-third of the pastry and use it to line a 20cm/8in pie tin 4cm/1¹/2in deep. Place on a baking sheet.

2 Mince 115g/4oz of the chicken with the gammon, then mix with the cream, spring onions, herbs, lemon rind, 15ml/1 tbsp of the lemon juice and the seasoning to make a soft mixture; add more cream if necessary.

3 Cut the remaining chicken into 1cm/¹/2in pieces and mix with the remaining lemon juice, the mace and seasoning.

4 Make a layer of one-third of the gammon mixture in the pastry base, cover with half the chopped chicken, then add another layer of one-third of the gammon. Add all the remaining chicken followed by the remaining gammon mixture.

5 Dampen the edges of the pastry base. Roll out the remaining two-thirds of the pastry to make a lid for the pie.

6 Use the trimmings to make a lattice decoration. Make a small hole in the centre of the pie, brush the top with beaten egg or milk, then bake for approximately 20 minutes. Reduce the oven temperature to 160°C/325°F/Gas 3 and bake for a further 1–1¹/4 hours; cover the top with foil if the pastry becomes too brown. Transfer the pie to a wire rack and leave to cool.

Chicken, Leek and Parsley Pie

*The flavours of chicken and leek
complement each other wonderfully.*

Serves 4–6
For the pastry
275g/10oz/2^1/2 cups plain flour
pinch of salt
200g/7oz/^{7}/8 cup butter, diced
2 egg yolks

For the filling
3 part-boned chicken breasts
flavouring ingredients e.g. bouquet garni,
    black peppercorns, onion and carrot
50g/2oz/4 tbsp butter
2 leeks, thinly sliced
50g/2oz/^{1}/2 cup Cheddar cheese, grated
25g/1oz/^{1}/3 cup Parmesan cheese, finely
    grated
45ml/3 tbsp chopped fresh parsley
30ml/2 tbsp wholegrain mustard
5ml/1 tsp cornflour
300ml/^{1}/2 pint/1^1/4 cups double cream
salt and black pepper
beaten egg, to glaze
mixed green salad, to serve

1 To make the pastry, first sift the
flour and salt. Blend together
the butter and egg yolks in a food
processor until creamy. Add the
flour and process until the mixture
is just coming together. Add about
15ml/1 tbsp cold water and process
for a few seconds more. Turn out
on to a lightly floured surface and
knead lightly. Wrap in clear film
and chill for about 1 hour.

2 Meanwhile, poach the chicken
breasts in water to cover, with
the flavouring ingredients added.
Cook the chicken until tender.
Leave to cool in the liquid.

3 Preheat the oven to 200°C/
400°F/Gas 6. Divide the pastry
into two pieces, one slightly larger
than the other. Roll out the larger
piece on a lightly floured surface
and use to line an 18 x 28cm/
7 x 11in baking dish or tin. Prick
the base with a fork and bake for
15 minutes. Leave to cool.

4 Lift the cooled chicken from
the poaching liquid and
discard the skins and bones. Cut
the chicken flesh into strips, then
set aside.

5 Melt the butter in a frying pan
and fry the sliced leeks over a
low heat, stirring occasionally,
until soft.

6 Stir in the Cheddar, Parmesan
and chopped parsley. Spread
half the leek mixture over the
cooked pastry base, leaving a
border all the way round.

7 Cover the leek mixture with
the chicken strips, then top
with the remaining leek mixture.
Mix together the wholegrain
mustard, cornflour and double
cream in a small bowl. Add
seasoning to taste. Pour over the
chicken and leek filling.

8 Moisten the edges of the
cooked pastry base. Roll out
the remaining pastry into a
rectangle and use to cover the pie.
Brush the lid of the pie with beaten
egg and bake in the preheated oven
for 30–40 minutes until the pie is
golden and crisp. Serve hot, cut
into generous square portions,
with a mixed green side salad.

Chicken Pastitsio

A traditional Greek pastitsio is a rich, high fat dish made with beef mince, but this lighter version with chicken is just as tasty.

Serves 4–6

450g/1lb lean minced chicken
1 large onion, finely chopped
60ml/4 tbsp tomato purée
250ml/8fl oz/1 cup red wine or stock
5ml/1 tsp ground cinnamon
300g/11oz/2^1/2 cups macaroni
300ml/^{1}/2 pint/1^1/4 cups milk
25g/1oz/2 tbsp sunflower margarine
25g/1oz/4 tbsp plain flour
5ml/1 tsp grated nutmeg
2 tomatoes, sliced
60ml/4 tbsp wholemeal breadcrumbs
salt and black pepper
green salad, to serve

1 Preheat the oven to 220°C/ 425°F/Gas 7. Fry the chicken and onion in a non-stick pan without fat, stirring until lightly browned.

2 Stir in the tomato purée, red wine or stock and cinnamon. Season, then cover and simmer for 5 minutes, stirring from time to time. Remove from the heat.

3 Cook the macaroni in plenty of boiling, salted water until just tender, then drain.

4 Layer the macaroni with the meat mixture in a wide ovenproof dish.

5 Place the milk, margarine and flour in a saucepan and whisk over a moderate heat until thickened and smooth. Add the nutmeg, and season to taste.

6 Pour the sauce evenly over the pasta and meat layers. Arrange the tomato slices on top and sprinkle lines of wholemeal breadcrumbs over the surface.

7 Bake for 30–35 minutes, or until golden brown and bubbling. Serve hot with a fresh green salad.

Chicken and Game Pie

A rich filling of chicken and dark meat, spiced with ginger.

INGREDIENTS

Serves 4

450g/1lb boneless chicken and game meat
   (plus the carcasses and bones)
1 small onion, halved
2 bay leaves
2 carrots, halved
a few black peppercorns
15ml/1 tbsp oil
75g/3oz streaky bacon pieces, rinded and
   chopped
15ml/1 tbsp plain flour
45ml/3 tbsp sweet sherry or Madeira
10ml/2 tsp ground ginger
grated rind and juice of $^1/_2$ orange
350g/12oz ready-made puff pastry
beaten egg or milk, to glaze
salt and black pepper

1 Place the carcasses and bones in a pan, with any giblets and half the onion, the bay leaves, carrots and black peppercorns. Cover with water and bring to the boil. Simmer until reduced to about 300ml/$^1/_2$ pint/1$^1/_4$ cups, then strain the stock, ready to use.

2 Cut the chicken and game meat into even-size pieces. Chop, then fry the remaining onion in the oil until softened. Then add the bacon and meat and fry quickly to seal. Sprinkle on the flour and stir until beginning to brown. Gradually add the stock, stirring as it thickens, then add the sherry or Madeira, ginger, orange rind and juice, and seasoning. Simmer for 20 minutes.

3 Transfer to a 900ml/1$^1/_2$ pints/ 3$^3/_4$ cups pie dish and allow to cool slightly. Use a pie funnel to help hold up the pastry.

4 Preheat the oven to 220°C/425°F/Gas 7. Roll out the pastry to 2.5cm/1in larger than the dish. Cut off a 1cm/$^1/_2$in strip all round. Dampen the rim of the dish and press on the strip of pastry. Dampen again and then lift the pastry carefully over the pie, sealing the edges well at the rim. Trim off the excess pastry, use to decorate the top, then brush the pie with egg or milk.

5 Bake for 15 minutes, then reduce the oven temperature to 190°C/375°F/Gas 5, for a further 25–30 minutes.

Chicken and Stilton Pies

These individual chicken and Stilton pies are wrapped in a crisp, shortcrust pastry and shaped into pasties. They are great for lunch, served hot or cold.

INGREDIENTS

Makes 4

350g/12oz/3 cups self-raising flour
2.5ml/¹/2 tsp salt
75g/3oz/6 tbsp lard
75g/3oz/6 tbsp butter
60–75ml/4–5 tbsp cold water
beaten egg, to glaze

For the filling
450g/1lb chicken thighs, boned and skinned
25g/1oz/¹/4 cup chopped walnuts
25g/1oz spring onions, sliced
50g/2oz/¹/2 cup Stilton, crumbled
25g/1oz celery, finely chopped
2.5ml/¹/2 tsp dried thyme
salt and black pepper

3 Remove any fat from the chicken thighs and cut into small cubes. Mix with the chopped walnuts, spring onions, Stilton, celery, thyme and seasoning and divide the filling equally among the four pastry circles.

4 Brush the edge of the pastry with beaten egg and fold over, pinching and crimping the edges together well. Place on a greased baking sheet and bake in the oven for about 45 minutes, or until golden brown.

1 Preheat the oven to 200°C/ 400°F/Gas 6. Mix the flour and salt in a bowl. Rub in the lard and butter with your fingers until the mixture resembles fine bread-crumbs. Using a knife to cut and stir, mix in the cold water to form a stiff, pliable dough.

2 Turn out on to a work surface and knead lightly until smooth. Divide into four and roll out each piece to a thickness of 5mm/¹/4in. Cut into a 20cm/8in circle.

Chicken Bouche

A spectacular centrepiece, this light pastry case contains a delicious chicken and mushroom filling with a hint of fruit. Ideal served with freshly cooked vegetables.

INGREDIENTS

Serves 4

450g/1lb ready-made puff pastry
beaten egg, to glaze

For the filling
15ml/1 tbsp oil
450g/1lb/3 cups minced chicken
25g/1oz/4 tbsp plain flour
150ml/^{1}/4 pint/^{2}/3 cup milk
150ml/^{1}/4 pint/^{2}/3 cup chicken
    stock
4 spring onions, chopped
25g/1oz/^{1}/4 cup redcurrants
75g/3oz button mushrooms, sliced
15ml/1 tbsp chopped fresh
    tarragon
salt and black pepper

1 Preheat the oven to 200°C/ 400°F/Gas 6. Roll half the pastry out on a lightly floured work surface to a 25cm/10in oval. Roll out the remainder to an oval of the same size and draw a smaller 20cm/8in oval in the centre.

2 Brush the edge of the first pastry shape with the beaten egg and place the smaller oval on top. Place on a dampened baking sheet and bake for 30 minutes.

3 For the filling, heat the oil in a large pan. Fry the minced chicken for 5 minutes. Add the flour and cook for a further 1 minute. Stir in the milk and stock and bring to the boil.

4 Add the spring onions, redcurrants and mushrooms. Cook for 20 minutes.

5 Stir in the fresh tarragon and season to taste.

6 Place the pastry bouche on a serving plate, remove the oval centre and spoon in the filling. Place the oval lid on top. Serve with freshly cooked vegetables.

VARIATION

You can also use shortcrust pastry for this dish and cook as a traditional chicken pie.

HOT & SPICY

Simple Curried Chicken

A tasty curry that needs very little preparation.

Serves 4

30ml/2 tbsp vegetable oil

1 onion, chopped

1 green or red pepper, seeded and diced

1 garlic clove, finely chopped

25ml/1^1/2 tbsp curry powder

2.5ml/^{1}/2 tsp dried thyme

450g/1lb tomatoes, skinned, seeded and chopped, or canned chopped tomatoes

30ml/2 tbsp lemon juice

120ml/4fl oz/^{1}/2 cup water

50g/2oz currants or raisins

salt and black pepper

1.5kg/3–3^1/2lb chicken, skinned and cut into 8 pieces

cooked rice, to serve

1 Preheat the oven to 180°C/ 350°F/Gas 4. Heat the vegetable oil in a wide, deep frying pan that has a lid and an ovenproof handle or in a flameproof casserole. Add the chopped onion, diced pepper and garlic. Cook, stirring occasionally, until the vegetables are soft but not too brown.

2 Stir in the curry powder and thyme, then add the tomatoes, lemon juice and water. Bring the sauce to the boil, stirring frequently. Stir in the currants or raisins. Season to taste with salt and pepper.

3 Put the chicken pieces in the frying pan or casserole, arranging them in one layer. Turn to coat them with the sauce. Cover the pan and transfer to the oven. Cook for about 40 minutes or until the chicken is tender. Turn the pieces halfway through cooking.

4 Remove the chicken and sauce to a warmed serving platter. Serve with freshly boiled rice.

VARIATION

For Curried Chicken Casserole, omit the diced pepper and cook 25ml/1^1/2 tbsp finely chopped fresh ginger and 1 green chilli, seeded and finely chopped, with the onion and garlic in a flameproof casserole. In step 3, stir in the curry powder with 450ml/^{3}/4 pint/ 1^3/4 cups natural yogurt; omit the tomatoes, lemon juice and water. Add the chicken pieces, cover and cook in the oven at a lower temperature of 160°C/325°F/Gas 3 for 1–1^1/4 hours.

Sour Chicken

There are few cookery concepts that are better suited to today's busy lifestyle than the all-in-one stir-fry. This one has a South-east Asian influence.

INGREDIENTS

Serves 4

275g/10oz Chinese egg noodles
30ml/2 tbsp vegetable oil
3 spring onions, chopped
1 garlic clove, crushed
2.5cm/1in piece fresh root ginger, peeled
   and grated
5ml/1 tsp hot paprika
5ml/1 tsp ground coriander
3 chicken breasts, boned and sliced
115g/4oz/1 cup sugar-snap peas, topped
   and tailed
115g/4oz baby corn on the cob, halved
225g/8oz fresh beansprouts
15ml/1 tbsp cornflour
45ml/3 tbsp soy sauce
45ml/3 tbsp lemon juice
15ml/1 tbsp sugar
45ml/3 tbsp chopped fresh coriander or
   spring onion tops, to garnish

1 Bring a large saucepan of salted water to the boil. Add the noodles and cook according to the instructions on the packet. Drain, cover and keep warm.

2 Heat the oil. Add the spring onions and cook over a gentle heat. Mix in the next five ingredients, then stir-fry for 3–4 minutes. Add the next three ingredients and steam briefly. Add the noodles.

3 Combine the cornflour, soy sauce, lemon juice and sugar in a small bowl. Add to the wok and simmer briefly to thicken. Serve garnished with chopped coriander or spring onion tops.

Chicken with Pineapple

This chicken has a delicate tang and is very tender. The pineapple not only tenderises the chicken but also gives it a slight sweetness.

Serves 6

225g/8oz can pineapple chunks
5ml/1 tsp ground cumin
5ml/1 tsp ground coriander
2.5ml/^{1}/$_2$ tsp crushed garlic
5ml/1 tsp chilli powder
5ml/1 tsp salt
30ml/2 tbsp natural yogurt
15ml/1 tbsp chopped fresh coriander
orange food colouring (optional)
275g/10oz chicken, skinned and boned
^{1}/$_2$ red pepper
^{1}/$_2$ yellow or green pepper
1 large onion
6 cherry tomatoes
15ml/1 tbsp vegetable oil

1 Drain the pineapple juice into a bowl. Reserve 8 large chunks of pineapple and squeeze the juice from the remaining chunks into the bowl and set aside. You should have about 120ml/4fl oz/^{1}/$_2$ cup pineapple juice.

2 In a large mixing bowl, blend together the cumin, ground coriander, garlic, chilli powder, salt, yogurt, fresh coriander and a few drops of food colouring, if using. Pour in the reserved pineapple juice and mix together.

3 Cut the chicken into bite-size cubes, add to the mixing bowl with the yogurt and spice mixture and leave to marinate for about 1–1^1/$_2$ hours.

4 Cut the peppers and onion into bite-size chunks.

COOK'S TIP
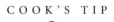
If possible, use a mixture of chicken breast and thigh meat for this recipe.

5 Preheat the grill to medium. Arrange the chicken pieces, peppers, onion, tomatoes and reserved pineapple chunks alternately on 6 wooden or metal skewers.

6 Baste the kebabs with the oil, then place the skewers on a flameproof dish or grill pan. Grill, turning and basting the chicken pieces with the marinade regularly, for about 15 minutes.

7 Once the chicken pieces are cooked, remove them from the grill and serve either with salad or plain boiled rice.

Chicken with Spiced Rice

This is a good dish for entertaining. It can be prepared in advance and reheated in the oven. Serve with traditional curry accompaniments.

Serves 8

900g/2lb boneless chicken thighs
60ml/4 tbsp olive oil
2 large onions, thinly sliced
1–2 green chillies, seeded and finely
    chopped
5ml/1 tsp grated fresh root ginger
1 garlic clove, crushed
15ml/1 tbsp hot curry powder
150ml/^{1}/4 pint/^{2}/3 cup chicken stock
150ml/^{1}/4 pint/^{2}/3 cup natural yogurt
30ml/2 tbsp chopped fresh coriander
salt and black pepper

For the spiced rice

450g/1lb/generous 2^1/4 cups basmati rice
2.5ml/^{1}/2 tsp garam masala
900ml/1^1/2 pints/3^3/4 cups chicken stock
    or water
50g/2oz/scant ^{1}/2 cup raisins or sultanas
25g/1oz/^{1}/2 cup toasted chopped
    almonds

1 Put the basmati rice into a sieve and wash under cold running water to remove any starchy powder coating the grains. Then put into a bowl and cover with cold water and leave to soak for 30 minutes. The grains will absorb some water so that they will not stick together in a solid mass while cooking.

2 Preheat the oven to 160°C/ 325°F/Gas 3. Cut the chicken into cubes of approximately 2.5cm/1in. Heat 30ml/2 tbsp of the oil in a large flameproof casserole, add one onion and cook until softened. Add the finely chopped chillies, ginger, garlic and curry powder and continue cooking for a further 2 minutes, stirring from time to time.

3 Add the stock and seasoning, bring slowly to the boil. Add the chicken. Cover and cook in the oven for 20 minutes or until tender.

4 Remove from the oven and stir in the yogurt.

5 Meanwhile, heat the remaining oil in a flameproof casserole and cook the remaining onion gently until tender and lightly browned. Add the drained rice, garam masala and stock or water. Bring to the boil, cover and cook in the oven with the chicken for 20–35 minutes or until tender and all the stock has been absorbed.

6 To serve, stir the raisins or sultanas and toasted almonds into the rice. Spoon half the rice into a large deep serving dish, cover with the chicken and then the remaining rice. Sprinkle with chopped coriander to garnish.

Hot Chicken Curry

This curry has a delicious thick sauce with extra colour provided by chunks of red and green pepper.

INGREDIENTS

Serves 4

30ml/2 tbsp corn oil

1.5ml/^{1}/$_4$ tsp fenugreek seeds

1.5ml/^{1}/$_4$ tsp onion seeds

2 onions, chopped

2.5ml/^{1}/$_2$ tsp chopped garlic

2.5ml/^{1}/$_2$ tsp chopped fresh root ginger

5ml/1 tsp ground coriander

5ml/1 tsp chilli powder

5ml/1 tsp salt

400g/14oz can tomatoes

30ml/2 tbsp lemon juice

350g/12oz/2^1/$_2$ cups cubed chicken

30ml/2 tbsp chopped fresh coriander

3 green chillies, chopped

^{1}/$_2$ red pepper, cut into chunks

^{1}/$_2$ green pepper, cut into chunks

sprigs fresh coriander, to garnish

1 In a medium saucepan, heat the oil and fry the fenugreek and onion seeds until they turn a shade darker. Add the chopped onions, garlic and ginger and fry for about 5 minutes until the onions turn golden brown. Reduce the heat to very low.

2 Meanwhile, in a separate bowl, mix together the ground coriander, chilli powder, salt, tomatoes and lemon juice.

3 Pour this mixture into the saucepan with the onions and increase the heat to medium. Stir-fry for about 3 minutes.

4 Add the chicken pieces and stir-fry for 5–7 minutes.

5 Add the coriander, chillies and peppers. Lower the heat, cover and simmer for 10 minutes until the chicken is cooked.

6 Serve hot, garnished with fresh coriander sprigs.

COOK'S TIP

For a milder version of this delicious curry, simply omit some or all of the green chillies.

San Francisco Chicken Wings

Make these as spicy as you like – just add more chilli sauce.

Serves 4

85ml/3fl oz/³/4 cup soy sauce
15ml/1 tbsp light brown sugar
15ml/1 tbsp rice vinegar
30ml/2 tbsp dry sherry
juice of 1 orange
5cm/2in strip orange rind
1 star anise
5ml/1 tsp cornflour
50ml/2fl oz/¹/4 cup water
15ml/1 tbsp minced fresh root ginger
1.5–5ml/¹/4–1 tsp Oriental chilli-garlic
   sauce, to taste
1.5kg/3–3¹/2lb chicken wings, about
   22–24, tips removed

1 Preheat the oven to 200°C/400°F/Gas 6. Combine the ingredients for the sauce: the soy sauce, light brown sugar, rice vinegar, dry sherry, orange juice and rind and star anise, in a saucepan. Bring to the boil over a medium heat.

2 Combine the cornflour and water in a small bowl and stir until blended. Add to the boiling soy sauce mixture, stirring well. Boil for a further 1 minute, stirring all the time.

3 Remove the soy sauce mixture from the heat and stir in the minced ginger and chilli-garlic sauce to taste.

4 Arrange the chicken wings, in one layer, in a large baking dish. Pour over the soy sauce mixture and stir to coat the wings evenly.

5 Bake until tender and browned, 30–40 minutes, basting occasionally. Serve the wings hot or warm.

Fragrant Chicken Curry

In this dish, the mildly spiced sauce is thickened using lentils rather than the traditional onions fried in ghee.

INGREDIENTS

Serves 4

75g/3oz/scant 1/2 cup red lentils

30ml/2 tbsp mild curry powder

10ml/2 tsp ground coriander

5ml/1 tsp cumin seeds

475ml/16fl oz/2 cups vegetable stock

8 chicken thighs, skinned

225g/8oz fresh shredded, or frozen
    spinach, thawed and well drained

15ml/1 tbsp chopped fresh coriander

salt and black pepper

sprigs of fresh coriander, to garnish

white or brown basmati rice and grilled
    poppadums, to serve

1 Rinse the lentils under cold running water. Put into a large, heavy-based saucepan with the curry powder, ground coriander, cumin seeds and stock.

2 Bring to the boil then lower the heat. Cover and simmer gently for 10 minutes.

3 Add the chicken and spinach. Cover and simmer gently for a further 40 minutes, or until the chicken is cooked.

4 Stir in the chopped coriander and season to taste. Serve garnished with fresh coriander and accompanied by the rice and grilled poppadums.

Spicy Masala Chicken

These chicken pieces are grilled and have a sweet-and-sour taste. They can be served cold with a salad and rice or hot with mashed potatoes.

INGREDIENTS

Serves 6

12 chicken thighs
90ml/6 tbsp lemon juice
5ml/1 tsp chopped fresh root ginger
5ml/1 tsp chopped garlic
5ml/1 tsp crushed dried red chillies
5ml/1 tsp salt
5ml/1 tsp soft brown sugar
30ml/2 tbsp clear honey
30ml/2 tbsp chopped fresh coriander
1 green chilli, finely chopped
30ml/2 tbsp vegetable oil
fresh coriander sprigs, to garnish

1 Prick the chicken thighs with a fork, rinse, pat dry and set aside in a bowl.

2 In a large mixing bowl, make the marinade by mixing together the lemon juice, ginger, garlic, crushed dried red chillies, salt, sugar and honey.

3 Transfer the chicken thighs to the spice mixture and coat well. Set aside for about 45 minutes.

4 Preheat the grill to medium. Add the fresh coriander and chopped green chilli to the chicken thighs and place them in a flame-proof dish.

5 Pour any remaining marinade over the chicken and baste with the oil.

6 Grill the chicken thighs under the preheated grill for about 15–20 minutes, turning and basting occasionally, until they are cooked through and browned.

7 Transfer the chicken to a serving dish and garnish with a few sprigs of fresh coriander.

Tandoori Chicken

A famous Indian/Pakistani chicken dish which is cooked in a clay oven called a tandoor, this is extremely popular in the West and appears on the majority of the restaurant menus. Though the authentic tandoori flavour is very difficult to achieve in conventional ovens, this version still makes a very tasty dish.

INGREDIENTS

Serves 4

4 chicken quarters

175ml/6fl oz/³/4 cup natural low-fat yogurt

5ml/1 tsp garam masala

5ml/1 tsp chopped fresh root ginger

5ml/1 tsp chopped garlic

7.5ml/1¹/2 tsp chilli powder

1.5ml/¹/4 tsp ground turmeric

5ml/1 tsp ground coriander

15ml/1 tbsp lemon juice

5ml/1 tsp salt

a few drops red food colouring

30ml/2 tbsp corn oil

To garnish

mixed salad leaves

lime wedges

1 tomato, quartered

1 Skin, rinse and pat dry the chicken quarters. Make 2 slits into the flesh of each piece, place in a dish and set aside.

2 Mix together the yogurt, garam masala, ginger, garlic, chilli powder, turmeric, ground coriander, lemon juice, salt, red food colouring and oil, and beat until well mixed together.

3 Cover the chicken quarters with the yogurt and spice mixture and leave to marinate for about 3 hours.

4 Preheat the oven to 240°C/ 475°F/Gas 9. Transfer the chicken pieces to an ovenproof dish.

5 Bake in the oven for about 20–25 minutes, or until the chicken is cooked right through and browned on top.

6 Remove from the oven, transfer to a serving dish and garnish with the salad leaves, lime and tomato.

Chicken Naan Pockets

This quick and easy dish is ideal for a speedy snack, lunch or supper. To save time, use the ready-to-bake naans available in some supermarkets and Asian stores, or try warmed pitta bread instead.

INGREDIENTS

Serves 4

4 ready-prepared naans
45ml/3 tbsp natural low-fat yogurt
7.5ml/1¹/2 tsp garam masala
5ml/1 tsp chilli powder
5ml/1 tsp salt
45ml/3 tbsp lemon juice
15ml/1 tbsp chopped fresh coriander
1 green chilli, chopped
450g/1lb/3¹/4 cups cubed chicken
15ml/1 tbsp vegetable oil (optional)
8 onion rings
2 tomatoes, quartered
¹/2 white cabbage, shredded

To garnish
lemon wedges
2 small tomatoes, halved
mixed salad leaves
fresh coriander

1 Cut into the middle of each naan to make a pocket, then set aside.

2 Mix together the yogurt, garam masala, chilli powder, salt, lemon juice, fresh coriander and chopped green chilli. Pour the marinade over the chicken pieces and leave them to marinate for about 1 hour.

3 Preheat the grill to very hot, then lower the heat to medium. Place the chicken in a flameproof dish and grill for 15–20 minutes until tender and cooked through, turning the chicken at least twice.

4 Remove from the heat and fill each naan with the chicken and then with the onion rings, tomatoes and cabbage. Serve with the garnish ingredients.

Chicken Tikka

This chicken dish is an extremely popular Indian appetizer and is quick and easy to cook. Chicken Tikka can also be served as a main course for four.

INGREDIENTS

Serves 6

450g/1lb/3¹/4 cups cubed chicken
5ml/1 tsp chopped fresh root ginger
5ml/1 tsp chopped garlic
5ml/1 tsp chilli powder
1.5ml/¹/4 tsp ground turmeric
5ml/1 tsp salt
150ml/¹/4 pint/²/3 cup natural low-fat yogurt
60ml/4 tbsp lemon juice
15ml/1 tbsp chopped fresh coriander
15ml/1 tbsp vegetable oil

To garnish
1 small onion, cut into rings
lime wedges
mixed salad
fresh coriander

1 In a medium bowl, mix together the chicken pieces, ginger, garlic, chilli powder, turmeric, salt, yogurt, lemon juice and fresh coriander and leave to marinate for at least 2 hours.

2 Place on a grill pan or in a flameproof dish lined with foil and baste with the oil.

3 Preheat the grill to medium. Grill the chicken for 15–20 minutes until cooked, turning and basting two or three times. Serve with the garnish ingredients.

Chicken in a Cashew Nut Sauce

This chicken dish has a deliciously thick and nutty sauce, and it is best served with plain boiled rice.

INGREDIENTS

Serves 4

2 onions
30ml/2 tbsp tomato purée
50g/2oz/^{1}/3 cup cashew nuts
7.5ml/1^1/2 tsp garam masala
5ml/1 tsp crushed garlic
5ml/1 tsp chilli powder
15ml/1 tbsp lemon juice
1.5ml/^{1}/4 tsp ground turmeric
5ml/1 tsp salt
15ml/1 tbsp natural low-fat yogurt
30ml/2 tbsp corn oil
15ml/1 tbsp chopped fresh coriander
15ml/1 tbsp sultanas
450g/1lb/3^1/4 cups cubed chicken
175g/6oz/2^1/4 cups button
    mushrooms
300ml/^{1}/2 pint/1^1/4 cups water
chopped fresh coriander, to garnish

3 In a saucepan, heat the oil, lower the heat to medium and pour in the spice mixture from the food processor. Fry for about 2 minutes, turning down the heat if necessary.

1 Cut the onions into quarters then place them in a food processor or blender and process for about 1 minute.

2 Add the tomato purée, cashew nuts, garam masala, garlic, chilli powder, lemon juice, turmeric, salt and yogurt. Process for a further 1–1^1/2 minutes.

4 Add the fresh coriander, sultanas and cubed chicken and continue to stir-fry for a further 1 minute.

5 Add the mushrooms, pour in the water and bring to a simmer. Cover and cook over a low heat for about 10 minutes, or until the chicken is cooked through and the sauce is thick. Cook for a little longer if necessary.

6 Serve garnished with chopped fresh coriander.

Chicken with Green Mango

Green, unripe mango is used for cooking various dishes on the Indian sub-continent, including pickles, chutneys and some meat, chicken and vegetable dishes. This is a fairly simple chicken dish to prepare and is served with rice and dhal.

INGREDIENTS

Serves 4

1 green mango
450g/1lb/3^1/4 cups cubed chicken
1.5ml/^{1}/4 tsp onion seeds
5ml/1 tsp grated fresh root ginger
2.5ml/^{1}/2 tsp crushed garlic
5ml/1 tsp chilli powder
1.5ml/^{1}/4 tsp ground turmeric
5ml/1 tsp salt
5ml/1 tsp ground coriander
30ml/2 tbsp corn oil
2 onions, sliced
4 curry leaves
300ml/^{1}/2 pint/1^1/4 cups water
2 tomatoes, quartered
2 green chillies, chopped
30ml/2 tbsp chopped fresh coriander

1 To prepare the mango, peel, stone and slice the flesh thickly. Place the mango slices in a small bowl, cover and set aside.

2 Place the chicken cubes in a bowl and add the onion seeds, ginger, garlic, chilli powder, turmeric, salt and ground coriander. Mix the spices into the chicken and then add half the mango slices.

3 In a medium saucepan, heat the oil and fry the sliced onions until they turn golden brown. Add the curry leaves.

4 Gradually add the spiced chicken pieces and mango slices, stirring all the time.

5 Pour in the water, lower the heat and cook for about 12–15 minutes, stirring occasionally, until the chicken is cooked through and the water has been absorbed.

6 Add the remaining mango slices, the tomatoes, green chillies and fresh coriander and serve hot.

Karahi Chicken with Mint

For this tasty dish, the chicken is first boiled before being quickly stir-fried in a little oil.

Serves 4

275g/10oz chicken breast fillet, skinned
    and cut into strips
300ml/^{1}/$_2$ pint/1^1/$_4$ cups water
30ml/2 tbsp soya oil
2 bunches spring onions, roughly
    chopped
5ml/1 tsp grated fresh root ginger
5ml/1 tsp crushed dried red chilli
30ml/2 tbsp lemon juice
15ml/1 tbsp chopped fresh coriander
15ml/1 tbsp chopped fresh mint
3 tomatoes, seeded and roughly chopped
5ml/1 tsp salt
mint and coriander sprigs, to garnish

1 Put the chicken and water into a saucepan, bring to the boil and lower the heat to medium. Cook for about 10 minutes or until the water has evaporated and the chicken is cooked. Remove from the heat and set aside.

2 Heat the oil in a frying pan or saucepan and stir-fry the spring onions for about 2 minutes until soft.

3 Add the boiled chicken strips to the pan and stir-fry them for about 3 minutes over a medium heat.

4 Gradually add the ginger, dried chilli, lemon juice, fresh coriander, fresh mint, tomatoes and salt and gently stir to blend all the flavours together.

5 Transfer to a serving dish and garnish with the fresh mint and coriander sprigs.

Karahi Chicken with Fresh Fenugreek

Fresh fenugreek is a flavour that not many people are familiar with and this recipe is a good introduction to this delicious herb.

INGREDIENTS

Serves 4

115g/4oz chicken thigh meat, skinned and cut into strips
115g/4oz chicken breast fillet, cut into strips
2.5ml/^{1}/$_2$ tsp chopped garlic
5ml/1 tsp chilli powder
2.5ml/^{1}/$_2$ tsp salt
10ml/2 tsp tomato purée
30ml/2 tbsp soya oil
1 bunch fenugreek leaves
15ml/1 tbsp chopped fresh coriander
300ml/^{1}/$_2$ pint/1^1/$_4$ cups water
rice or chapatis, to serve

1 Bring a saucepan of water to the boil, add the chicken and cook for 5–7 minutes. Drain.

3 Heat the oil in a large saucepan. Lower the heat and add the tomato purée and spice mixture.

5 Add the fenugreek leaves and fresh coriander. Continue to stir-fry for 5–7 minutes.

6 Pour in the water, cover and cook for about 5 minutes and serve hot with rice or chapatis.

2 In a mixing bowl, combine the garlic, chilli powder and salt with the tomato purée.

4 Add the chicken pieces and stir-fry for 5–7 minutes. Lower the heat again.

COOK'S TIP

When preparing fresh fenugreek, use only the leaves and discard the stems which are very bitter.

Moroccan Chicken Couscous

A subtly spiced and fragrant dish with a fruity sauce.

Serves 4

15ml/1 tbsp butter
15ml/1 tbsp sunflower oil
4 chicken portions, about 175g/6oz each
2 onions, finely chopped
2 garlic cloves, crushed
2.5ml/^{1}/$_2$ tsp ground cinnamon
1.5ml/^{1}/$_4$ tsp ground ginger
1.5ml/^{1}/$_4$ tsp ground turmeric
30ml/2 tbsp orange juice
10ml/2 tsp clear honey
salt
fresh mint sprigs, to garnish

For the couscous

350g/12oz/2 cups couscous
5ml/1 tsp salt
10ml/2 tsp caster sugar
30ml/2 tbsp sunflower oil
2.5ml/^{1}/$_2$ tsp ground cinnamon
pinch of grated nutmeg
15ml/1 tbsp orange flower water
30ml/2 tbsp sultanas
50g/2oz/^{1}/$_2$ cup chopped blanched
    almonds
45ml/3 tbsp chopped pistachios

1 Heat the butter and oil in a large pan and add the chicken portions, skin-side down. Fry for 3–4 minutes, until the skin is golden, then turn over.

2 Add the onions, garlic, spices and a pinch of salt and pour over the orange juice and 300ml/^{1}/$_2$ pint/1^1/$_4$ cups water. Cover and bring to the boil, then reduce the heat and simmer for about 30 minutes.

3 Meanwhile, place the couscous and salt in a bowl and cover with 350ml/12fl oz/1^1/$_2$ cups water. Stir once and leave to stand for 5 minutes. Add the caster sugar, 15ml/1 tbsp of the oil, the cinnamon, nutmeg, orange flower water and sultanas and mix well.

4 Heat the remaining 15ml/1 tbsp of the oil in a pan and lightly fry the almonds until golden. Stir into the couscous with the pistachios.

5 Line a steamer with grease-proof paper and spoon in the couscous. Sit the steamer over the chicken (or over a pan of boiling water) and steam for 10 minutes.

6 Remove the steamer and keep covered. Stir the honey into the chicken liquid and boil rapidly for 3–4 minutes. Spoon the couscous on to a warmed serving platter and top with the chicken, with a little of the sauce spooned over. Garnish with fresh mint and serve with the remaining sauce.

Chicken and Chorizo Tacos

Use bought taco shells and fill with tasty minced chicken.

Serves 4

15ml/1 tbsp vegetable oil

450g/1lb minced chicken

5ml/1 tsp salt

5ml/1 tsp ground cumin

12 taco shells

75g/3oz chorizo sausage, minced

3 spring onions, chopped

2 tomatoes, chopped

1/2 head of lettuce, shredded

225g/8oz/2 cups grated Cheddar cheese

tomato salsa, to serve

1 Preheat the oven to 180°C/ 350°F/Gas 4.

2 Heat the oil in a non-stick frying pan. Add the chicken, salt and cumin and fry over a medium heat until the chicken is cooked through, 5–8 minutes. Stir frequently to prevent large lumps from forming.

3 Meanwhile, arrange the taco shells in one layer on a large baking sheet and heat in the oven for about 10 minutes, or according to the directions on the packet.

4 Add the chorizo and spring onions to the chicken and stir to mix. Cook until just warmed through, stirring occasionally.

5 To assemble each taco, place 1–2 spoonfuls of the chicken mixture in the base of a warmed taco shell. Top with a generous sprinkling of chopped tomato, shredded lettuce, and grated cheese.

6 Serve immediately, with tomato salsa to accompany.

Chicken Pilau

This dish is a complete meal on its own, but also makes a good accompaniment to curries.

Serves 4

400g/14oz/2 cups basmati rice
75g/3oz/6 tbsp low-fat margarine
1 onion, sliced
1.5ml/^{1}/$_4$ tsp mixed onion and mustard
   seeds
3 curry leaves
5ml/1 tsp grated fresh root ginger
5ml/1 tsp crushed garlic
5ml/1 tsp ground coriander
5ml/1 tsp chilli powder
7.5ml/1^1/$_2$ tsp salt
2 tomatoes, sliced
1 potato, cubed
50g/2oz/^{1}/$_2$ cup frozen peas
175g/6oz/1^1/$_4$ cups cubed chicken
60ml/4 tbsp chopped fresh coriander
2 green chillies, chopped
750ml/1^1/$_4$ pints/3 cups water

1 Wash and soak the rice in plenty of cold water for 30 minutes, then set aside in a sieve.

2 In a medium saucepan, melt the low-fat margarine and fry the sliced onion until golden.

3 Add the onion and mustard seeds, the curry leaves, ginger, garlic, ground coriander, chilli powder and salt. Stir-fry for about 2 minutes.

4 Add the sliced tomatoes, cubed potato, peas and chicken and mix well.

5 Add the drained rice and stir gently to combine with the other ingredients.

6 Finally, add the fresh coriander and chopped green chillies. Mix and stir-fry for a further 1 minute. Pour in the water.

7 Bring to the boil and lower the heat. Cover and cook for about 20 minutes.

Cajun Chicken

Use cooked ham and prawns if you have them, but chicken and chorizo sausage are the main ingredients for this dish.

Serves 4

1.25kg/2^1/2 lb fresh chicken
1^1/2 onions
1 bay leaf
4 black peppercorns
1 parsley sprig
30ml/2 tbsp vegetable oil
2 garlic cloves, chopped
1 green pepper, seeded and chopped
1 celery stick, chopped
225g/8oz/1^1/4 cups long grain rice
115g/4oz/1 cup chorizo sausage, sliced
115g/4oz/1 cup chopped, cooked ham
400g/14oz can chopped tomatoes with
    herbs
2.5ml/^{1}/2 tsp hot chilli powder
2.5ml/^{1}/2 tsp cumin seeds
2.5ml/^{1}/2 tsp ground cumin
5ml/1 tsp dried thyme
115g/4oz/1 cup cooked, peeled prawns
dash of Tabasco sauce
chopped parsley, to garnish

1 Place the chicken in a large flameproof casserole and pour over 600ml/1 pint/2^1/2 cups water. Add the half onion, the bay leaf, peppercorns and parsley and bring to the boil. Cover and simmer gently for about 1^1/2 hours.

2 When the chicken is cooked lift it out of the stock, remove the skin and carcass and chop the meat. Strain the stock, leave to cool and reserve.

3 Chop the remaining onion and heat the oil in a large frying pan. Add the onion, garlic, green pepper and celery. Fry for about 5 minutes, then stir in the rice coating the grains with the oil. Add the sausage, ham and reserved chopped chicken and fry for a further 2–3 minutes, stirring frequently.

4 Pour in the tomatoes and 300ml/^{1}/2 pint/1^1/4 cups of the reserved stock and add the chilli, cumin and thyme. Bring to the boil, then cover and simmer gently for 20 minutes, or until the rice is tender and the liquid absorbed.

5 Stir in the prawns and Tabasco. Cook for a further 5 minutes, then season well and serve hot garnished with chopped parsley.

Galveston Chicken

An American favourite, crisp roasted chicken with garlic.

INGREDIENTS

Serves 4

1.5kg/3–3^1/2lb chicken

juice of 1 lemon

4 garlic cloves, crushed

15ml/1 tbsp cayenne pepper

15ml/1 tbsp paprika

15ml/1 tbsp dried oregano

2.5ml/^{1}/2 tsp coarse black pepper

10ml/2 tsp olive oil

5ml/1 tsp salt

1 With a sharp knife or poultry shears, remove the backbone from the chicken. Turn it breast side up. With the heel of your hand, press down to break the breastbone, and open the chicken flat like a book. Insert a skewer through the chicken, at the thighs, to keep it flat during cooking.

2 Place the chicken in a shallow dish and pour over the lemon juice to coat.

3 In a small bowl, combine the garlic, cayenne, paprika, oregano, pepper and oil. Mix well. Rub evenly over the surface of the chicken.

4 Cover and let marinate 2–3 hours at room temperature, or chill overnight (return to room temperature before roasting).

5 Season the chicken with salt on both sides. Transfer it to a shallow roasting pan.

6 Put the pan in a cold oven and set the temperature to 200°C/ 400°F/Gas 6. Roast until the chicken is done, about 1 hour, turning occasionally and basting with the pan juices. To test, prick with a skewer: the juices that run out should be clear.

> COOK'S TIP
>
> ❧
>
> Roasting chicken in an oven that has not been preheated produces a particularly crispy skin.

Indian Spiced Chicken

*Tender marinated chicken pieces
which can be served hot or cold.*

Serves 4

1.75kg/4–4^1/2lb chicken

mixed salad leaves, e.g. frisée and oakleaf
    lettuce or radicchio, to serve

For the marinade

150ml/^{1}/4 pint/^{2}/3 cup plain low-fat
    yogurt

5ml/1 tsp ground paprika

10ml/2 tsp grated fresh root ginger

1 garlic clove, crushed

10ml/2 tsp garam masala

2.5ml/^{1}/2 tsp salt

red food colouring (optional)

juice of 1 lemon

1 Joint the chicken and divide it
into 8 pieces, using a sharp
knife.

2 Mix the marinade ingredients
in a large dish, add the chicken
pieces to coat and chill for 4 hours
or overnight to allow the flavours
to penetrate the flesh.

3 Preheat the oven to
200°C/400°F/Gas 6. Remove
the chicken pieces from the
marinade and arrange them in a
single layer in a large ovenproof
dish. Bake for 30–40 minutes or
until tender. Reserve the marinade.

4 Baste with a little of the
marinade while cooking.
Arrange on a bed of salad leaves
and serve hot or cold.

Chilli Chicken

*Serve as a simple supper dish with
boiled potatoes and broccoli, or as a
party dish with rice.*

Serves 4

12 chicken thighs

15ml/1 tbsp olive oil

1 onion, thinly sliced

1 garlic clove, crushed

5ml/1 tsp chilli powder or 1 red chilli,
    chopped

400g/14oz can chopped tomatoes, with
    the juice

5ml/1 tsp caster sugar

425g/15oz can red kidney beans, drained

salt and black pepper

1 Cut the chicken into large
cubes, removing all skin and
bones. Heat the oil in a large
flameproof casserole and brown
the chicken pieces on all sides.
Remove with a slotted spoon and
keep warm.

2 Add the onion and garlic to the
casserole and cook gently until
soft. Stir in the chilli powder or
chopped red chilli and cook for
2 minutes. Add the tomatoes with
their juice, seasoning and sugar.
Bring to the boil.

3 Replace the chicken pieces,
cover the casserole and simmer
for about 30 minutes until tender.

4 Add the red kidney beans and
gently cook for a further
5 minutes to heat them through
before serving.

Red-hot Chicken

A good party dish. The chicken is marinated the night before so all you have to do on the day is to cook it in a very hot oven and serve with wedges of lemon and a green salad.

INGREDIENTS

Serves 4

1.75kg/4–4¹/₂lb chicken, cut into 8 pieces

juice of 1 large lemon

150ml/¹/₄ pint/²/₃ cup natural low-fat yogurt

3 garlic cloves, crushed

30ml/2 tbsp olive oil

5ml/1 tsp ground turmeric

10ml/2 tsp paprika

5ml/1 tsp grated fresh root ginger or 2.5ml/¹/₂ tsp ground ginger

10ml/2 tsp garam masala

5ml/1 tsp salt

a few drops red food colouring (optional)

3 Mix together the remaining ingredients and pour the sauce over the chicken pieces, turning them to coat thoroughly. Cover with clear film and chill overnight.

4 Preheat the oven to 220°C/ 425°F/Gas 7. Remove the chicken from the marinade and arrange in a single layer on a shallow baking sheet. Bake for 15 minutes, turn over, and cook for a further 15 minutes or until tender.

1 Skin the chicken pieces and cut two slits in each piece.

2 Arrange in a single layer in a glass or ceramic dish and pour over the lemon juice.

Chinese Chicken Wings

These are best eaten with fingers as a starter. Make sure you provide finger bowls and plenty of paper napkins, it could get messy.

Serves 4

12 chicken wings
3 garlic cloves, crushed
4cm/1¹/₂in piece fresh root ginger, grated
juice of 1 large lemon
45ml/3 tbsp soy sauce
45ml/3 tbsp clear honey
2.5ml/¹/₂ tsp chilli powder
150ml/¹/₄ pint/²/₃ cup chicken stock
salt and black pepper
lemon wedges, to garnish

3 Preheat the oven to 220°C/ 425°F/Gas 7. Remove the wings from the marinade and arrange in a single layer in a roasting tin. Bake for 20–25 minutes, basting at least twice with the marinade during cooking.

4 Place the wings on a serving plate. Add the stock to the marinade in the roasting tin, and bring to the boil. Cook to a syrupy consistency and spoon a little over the wings. Serve garnished with lemon wedges.

1 Remove the wing tips and use to make the stock. Cut the wings into two pieces.

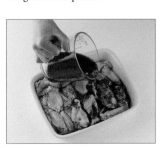

2 Mix the remaining ingredients, apart from the stock, together and coat the chicken pieces in the mixture. Cover with clear film and marinate overnight.

Moroccan Spiced Roast Poussin

Half poussins served with an apricot and rice stuffing.

Serves 4

75g/3oz/generous 1 cup cooked long grain
    rice
1 small onion, chopped finely
finely grated rind and juice of 1 lemon
30ml/2 tbsp chopped mint
45ml/3 tbsp chopped dried apricots
30ml/2 tbsp natural yogurt
10ml/2 tsp ground turmeric
10ml/2 tsp ground cumin
2 x 450g/1lb poussins
salt and black pepper
lemon slices and mint sprigs, to garnish

1 Preheat the oven to 200°C/
400°F/Gas 6. Mix together the
rice, onion, lemon rind, mint and
apricots. Stir in half each of the
lemon juice, yogurt, turmeric,
cumin, and salt and pepper.

2 Stuff the poussins with the rice
mixture at the neck end only.
Any spare stuffing can be served
separately. Place the poussins on a
rack in a roasting tin.

3 Mix together the remaining
lemon juice, yogurt, turmeric
and cumin, then brush over the
poussins. Cover loosely with foil
and cook the birds in the oven for
30 minutes.

4 Remove the foil and roast for a
further 15 minutes, or until
golden brown and the juices run
clear, not pink, when pierced.

5 Cut the poussins in half with a
sharp knife or poultry shears,
and serve with the spare rice.
Garnish with lemon slices and
fresh mint sprigs.

Sticky Ginger Chicken

*The sweet glaze turns dark and
sticky under the grill.*

Serves 4

30ml/2 tbsp lemon juice
30ml/2 tbsp muscovado sugar
5ml/1 tsp grated fresh root ginger
10ml/2 tsp soy sauce
8 chicken drumsticks, skinned
black pepper
lettuce and crusty bread, to serve

1 Mix together the lemon juice,
muscovado sugar, grated
ginger, soy sauce and pepper.

2 With a sharp knife, slash the
chicken drumsticks about three
times through the thickest part,
then toss the chicken in the glaze.

3 Cook the chicken drumsticks
under a hot grill or on a
barbecue, turning occasionally and
brushing with the glaze, until the
chicken is dark gold and the juices
run clear, not pink, when pierced
with a skewer. Serve on a bed of
lettuce with crusty bread, if you like.

Spatchcocked Devilled Poussins

"Spatchcock", perhaps a corruption of the old Irish phrase "despatch a cock", refers to birds that are split and skewered flat for cooking.

INGREDIENTS

Serves 4

15ml/1 tbsp English mustard powder
15ml/1 tbsp paprika
15ml/1 tbsp ground cumin
20ml/4 tsp tomato ketchup
15ml/1 tbsp lemon juice
65g/2¹/₂oz/5 tbsp butter, melted
4 poussins, about 450g/1lb each
salt

2 Using game shears or strong kitchen scissors, split each poussin along one side of the backbone, then cut down the other side of the backbone to remove it.

3 Open out a poussin, skin side uppermost, then press down firmly with the heel of your hand. Pass a long skewer through one leg and out through the other to secure the bird open and flat. Repeat with the remaining birds.

1 Mix together the mustard, paprika, cumin, ketchup, lemon juice and salt until smooth, then gradually stir in the butter.

4 Spread the mustard mixture evenly over the skin of the birds. Cover loosely and leave in a cool place for at least 2 hours. Preheat the grill.

5 Place the birds, skin side up, under the grill and cook for about 12 minutes. Turn over, baste and cook for a further 7 minutes, until the juices run clear.

COOK'S TIP
Spatchcocked poussins cook well on the barbecue. Make sure the coals are hot, then cook for 15–20 minutes, turning and basting frequently.

Sweet-spiced Chicken

*Make sure you allow plenty of time
for the chicken wings to marinate
so the flavours develop well, then
use a wok or a large frying pan for
stir-frying.*

INGREDIENTS

Serves 4

1 red chilli, finely chopped

5ml/1 tsp chilli powder

5ml/1 tsp ground ginger

rind of 1 lime, finely grated

12 chicken wings

60ml/2fl oz/^{1}/4 cup sunflower oil

15ml/1 tbsp fresh coriander, chopped

30ml/2 tbsp soy sauce

50ml/3^1/2 tbsp clear honey

lime rind and fresh coriander sprigs, to
    garnish

1 Mix the fresh chilli, chilli
powder, ground ginger and
lime rind together. Rub the
mixture into the chicken skins and
leave for at least 2 hours to allow
the flavours to penetrate.

2 Heat a wok or large frying pan
and add half of the oil. When
the oil is hot, add half the wings
and stir-fry for 10 minutes,
turning regularly until crisp and
golden. Drain on kitchen paper.
Repeat with the remaining wings.

3 Add the coriander to the hot
wok and stir-fry for 30
seconds, then return the wings to
the wok and stir-fry for 1 minute.

4 Stir in the soy sauce and
honey, and stir-fry for 1
minute. Serve the chicken wings
hot with the sauce drizzled over
them, garnished with lime rind
and coriander sprigs.

Quick Chicken Curry

Curry powder can be bought in three different strengths – mild, medium and hot. Use the type you prefer to suit your taste.

INGREDIENTS

Serves 4

8 chicken legs (thighs and drumsticks)
30ml/2 tbsp vegetable oil
1 onion, thinly sliced
1 garlic clove, crushed
15ml/1 tbsp curry powder
15ml/1 tbsp plain flour
450ml/^{3}/4 pint/1^3/4 cups chicken stock
1 beefsteak tomato
15ml/1 tbsp mango chutney
15ml/1 tbsp lemon juice
salt and black pepper
plain boiled rice, to serve

1 Cut the chicken legs in half. Heat the oil in a large flame-proof casserole and brown the chicken pieces on all sides. Remove and keep warm.

2 Add the onion and crushed garlic to the casserole and cook until soft. Add the curry powder and cook gently for 2 minutes.

3 Add the flour, and gradually blend in the chicken stock and the seasoning.

4 Bring to the boil, replace the chicken pieces, cover and simmer for 20–30 minutes or until tender.

5 Skin the tomato by blanching in boiling water for 45 seconds, then run under cold water to loosen the skin. Peel and cut into small cubes.

6 Add to the chicken, with the mango chutney and lemon juice. Heat through gently and adjust the seasoning to taste. Serve with plenty of boiled rice and Indian pickles.

Chicken in Green Almond Sauce

This casserole with its spicy sauce originates from Mexico.

Serves 6

1.5kg/3–3¹/₂lb chicken, cut into serving
    pieces
475ml/16fl oz/2 cups chicken stock
1 onion, chopped
1 garlic clove, chopped
115g/4oz/2 cups fresh coriander, coarsely
    chopped
1 green pepper, seeded and chopped
1 *jalapeño* chilli, seeded and chopped
275g/10oz can tomatillos (Mexican
    green tomatoes)
115g/4oz/1 cup ground almonds
30ml/2 tbsp corn oil
salt
fresh coriander sprig, to garnish
rice, to serve

1 Put the chicken pieces into a flameproof casserole or shallow pan. Pour in the stock, bring to a simmer, cover and cook for about 45 minutes, until tender. Drain the stock into a measuring jug and set aside.

2 Put the onion, garlic, coriander, green pepper, chilli, tomatillos with their juice and the almonds in a food processor. Purée fairly coarsely.

3 Heat the oil in a frying pan, add the almond mixture and cook over a low heat, stirring with a wooden spoon, for 3–4 minutes. Scrape into the casserole or pan with the chicken.

4 Make the stock up to 475ml/16fl oz/2 cups with water, if necessary. Stir it into the casserole or pan. Mix gently and simmer just long enough to blend the flavours and heat the chicken pieces through. Add salt to taste. Serve at once, garnished with coriander and accompanied by rice.

COOK'S TIP

If the colour of the sauce seems a little pale, add 2–3 outer leaves of dark green cos lettuce. Cut out the central veins, chop the leaves and add at step 2.

Chicken Bobotie

Perfect for a buffet party, this mild curry dish is set with savoury custard, which makes serving easy. Serve with boiled rice and chutney.

INGREDIENTS

Serves 8

two thick slices white bread

450ml/³/4 pint/1³/4 cups milk

30ml/2 tbsp olive oil

2 medium onions, finely chopped

45ml/3 tbsp medium curry powder

1.25kg/2¹/2lb minced raw chicken

15ml/1 tbsp apricot jam, chutney or caster sugar

30ml/2 tbsp wine vinegar or lemon juice

3 size 4 eggs, beaten

50g/2oz/¹/3 cup raisins or sultanas

12 whole almonds

salt and black pepper

1 Preheat the oven to 180°C/ 350°F/Gas 4. Soak the bread in 150ml/¹/4 pint/²/3 cup of the milk. Heat the oil in a frying pan and gently fry the onions until tender, then add the curry powder and cook for a further 2 minutes.

2 Add the minced chicken and brown all over, separating the grains of meat as they brown. Remove from the heat, season with salt and black pepper, add the apricot jam, chutney or caster sugar and the wine vinegar or lemon juice.

3 Mash the bread in the milk and add to the pan with one of the beaten eggs and the raisins.

4 Grease a 1.5 litre/2¹/2 pints/ 6¹/4 cups shallow ovenproof dish with butter. Spoon in the chicken mixture and level the top. Cover with buttered foil and bake in the oven for 30 minutes.

5 Meanwhile, beat the remaining eggs and milk. Remove the dish from the oven and lower the temperature to 150°C/300°F/Gas 2. Break up the meat using a fork and pour over the egg.

6 Scatter the almonds over and bake, uncovered, for 30 minutes until set and brown.

Chicken Biryani

A deceptively easy curry to make, and very tasty, too.

Serves 4

275g/10oz/1^1/2 cups basmati rice, rinsed

2.5ml/^{1}/2 tsp salt

5 whole cardamom pods

2–3 whole cloves

1 cinnamon stick

45ml/3 tbsp vegetable oil

3 onions, sliced

675g/1^1/2lb chicken (4 x 175g/6oz chicken breasts), cubed, skinned and boned

1.5ml/^{1}/4 tsp ground cloves

5 cardamom pods, seeds removed and ground

1.5ml/^{1}/4 tsp hot chilli powder

5ml/1 tsp ground cumin

5ml/1 tsp ground coriander

2.5ml/^{1}/2 tsp black pepper

3 garlic cloves, finely chopped

5ml/1 tsp finely chopped fresh root ginger

juice of 1 lemon

4 tomatoes, sliced

30ml/2 tbsp chopped fresh coriander

150ml/^{1}/4 pint/^{2}/3 cup natural yogurt

2.5ml/^{1}/2 tsp saffron strands soaked in 10ml/2 tsp hot milk

45ml/3 tbsp toasted flaked almonds and fresh coriander sprigs, to garnish

natural yogurt, to serve

1 Preheat the oven to 190°C/ 375°F/Gas 5. Bring a pan of water to the boil and add the rice, salt, cardamom pods, cloves and cinnamon stick. Boil for 2 minutes and then drain, leaving the whole spices in the rice.

2 Heat the oil in a pan and fry the onions for 8 minutes, until browned. Add the chicken followed by all the ground spices, the garlic, ginger and lemon juice. Stir-fry for 5 minutes.

3 Transfer the chicken mixture to a casserole and lay the sliced tomatoes on top. Sprinkle over the fresh coriander, spoon over the natural yogurt and top with the drained rice.

4 Drizzle the saffron and milk over the rice and pour over 150ml/^{1}/4 pint/^{2}/3 cup of water.

5 Cover tightly and bake in the oven for 1 hour. Transfer to a warmed serving platter and remove the whole spices from the rice. Garnish with toasted almonds and fresh coriander and serve with extra natural yogurt.

Index

NOTES

NOTES

NOTES

NOTES

NOTES

Notes

NOTES

NOTES